Steve Yzerman

Heart *of a* Champion

By Joe Falls,

Vartan Kupelian,

Cynthia Lambert,

John U. Bacon and

Terry Foster

Edited by

Francis J. Fitzgerald

Published by

Louisville, Ky.

From the Sports Pages of

The Detroit News

Acknowledgments

Research Assistance: *The Detroit News* library; The Detroit Red Wings Media Relations Office; Alan Whitt and Jefferey M. Samoray.

Photo Research: Steve Fecht, *The Detroit News*; Wide World Photos and Allsport Photography USA.

Production Assistance: Susan Kordalski and Philip K. Webb.

First Printing: December 1996
Second Printing: February 1997

ISBN 1-887761-14-4

Cover and Book Design by David Kordalski, Detroit.
Typefaces: Life and Berkeley

Published by:
AdCraft Sports Marketing Inc.
Kaden Tower, 10th Floor
6100 Dutchmans Lane
Louisville, Ky 40205
(502) 473-1124

This book is dedicated to
the memory of Elysia Pefley, one of Steve Yzerman's biggest fans.

Royalties from the sale of this book will benefit the
Michigan Cancer Foundation
and the Elysia Pefley Dance Scholarship Fund.

Contents

Introduction

The Captain Doesn't Quit

By Joe Falls

The Detroit News

How many times, in how many places, did we see Steve Yzerman sitting in front of his locker after the final game of the season, his head down, sweat running from his face onto his pants, speaking so softly it was almost impossible to hear him?

Or catching him outside the dressing room, in a hallway under the arena, still in his skates and appearing taller than the rest of us, his eyes straight ahead — empty eyes — trying, one more time, to explain this final loss of the season for the Detroit Red Wings?

Who hasn't hurt for Steve Yzerman?

But know one thing about this man. Actually, two things:

He never ducked the media. He always spoke to us, no matter how difficult things were for his hockey team. You could see the pain in his eyes and hear it in his voice. One more empty summer. One more summer of soul searching. What went wrong? How can it be changed? Will the pain ever go away? You had to lean in close to hear him. The words were barely audible at times. They put their microphones against his lips to pick up every syllable. Those of us in the back of the mob around his locker stood on our toes and turned our heads sideways to listen to him. The words were always there — soft, sad and sentimental. He is not a wordsmith, but a hockey player, and he did his best to help us.

He never blamed anyone for the troubles of his team.

If Bobby Layne was the heart of the Detroit Lions, Al Kaline the heart of the Tigers and Isiah Thomas the heart of the Pistons, then Gordie Howe was the heart of the Red Wings. No. 9 will always be No. 1. But No. 1-A is Steve Yzerman, the man who has given us so much of himself, year after year, frustration after frustration, never letting down, never dogging it, always trying to do better.

They want him to play center, he plays center. They want him out on the wing, he goes out on the wing.

Offense, defense ... it doesn't matter. He does it well and he does it for his team, and so there is little wonder that today he really is the Detroit Red Wings. If he has been booed — and I guess he has because everyone (except Barry Sanders) gets booed in this town, I have not been there to see it.

That makes me one of the lucky ones because this man is one of the pure athletes of our time — a man who does it all for his team and does it without complaint.

No wonder he is such a crowd favorite. They watch him and know that even when he is having his troubles, he keeps giving his best. He has captured their hearts by giving them his own heart. How can anyone not like Steve Yzerman, The Captain?

They have brought in Europeans — the rousing Russians. They've had tough guys and rough guys. Say hello to Bob Probert and Joey Kocur. They signed youngsters, oldsters, bought players, sold players — and even changed coaches.

The one constant has been Steve Yzerman, a man who has been asked to do much in our town — probably too much.

He knows what the Red Wings did to him in those early years. They all but burned him out by playing him so much. He was their only offensive weapon and they called on him again and again.

Yzerman didn't mind. As a young man, he loved his ice time. They all do. It is their life's blood. But with each game, each season, the toll grew greater and greater. It was hard to see — hard to recognize — but he slowed a little here, slowed a little there. he got nicked, then severely hurt, and the whole process became more demanding than ever.

Still, not a word of complaint.

Scotty Bowman, a late comer to our city, probably has the best insight of all to this man.

Bowman recognized what had happened to this wonderful player, so he knew he had to help him. He played him a little less. He used him more judiciously. Yzerman became a superb two-way player. More of a team player than ever.

And today, we see the product of a life of dedication. We see a man who understands himself and what he is trying to do in his profession. We have loved his cannon shots. Personally, I don't know why he hasn't scored more goals. He is forever coming in from the side of the net and letting that cannon shot go. Too many times the puck never found the back of the net. I figure he was good for 80 goals one of those years.

But it was not to be ... 50, 58, 62, 68 were plenty good enough, though. Again, it doesn't matter.

He was more than a man to be measured by statistics. He was No. 19, there for us all the time, coming out before the game and capturing our attention as he circled the ice. He always seemed to skate fast — faster than the others. What he was doing was testing himself — pushing himself.

He has been ours since 1983, but at some point down the road he won't be ours anymore. He is only 30 but this game has a way of taking a toll on a man's legs. Eventually, they will hoist his number to the ceiling, next to Gordie, Ted, Alex and Sid, and his place of honor will be fixed forever.

But, happily, he is still with us. Those cannon balls can still roll off his stick ... and, who knows, maybe one night in June, he will be standing in the middle of the dressing room and squirting champagne at everyone around him. And his voice will be loud. Maybe it'll be raucous. Even a little profane.

Who can deny him this moment?

Enjoy him. You don't get many like him in an entire lifetime.

Chapter One

The Making of a Superstar

By John U. Bacon

....

In September 1996, Team Canada played against seven other nations in the inaugural World Cup of Hockey tournament. Although he had been inexplicably cut from two previous national teams, Steve Yzerman was finally wearing Team Canada's red maple leaf again.

He skated on the fourth line, but he and his linemates were remarkably productive, often making the difference in big games against Sweden, Russia and the United States. In the first game of the best-of-three final series against the U.S., Yzerman scored the overtime goal that put his countrymen one game away from clinching the coveted title.

But something went terribly awry just before he could savor the rewards of his work. The U.S. shocked the hockey world by winning games 2 and 3, the latter in an improbable comeback to claim world supremacy.

The tournament was a microcosm of Yzerman's Job-like career: He overcame unappre-

ciative coaches with his selfless, gutsy play, only to see bad breaks turn his moment of triumph into another agonizing disappointment.

Although Yzerman will never surpass the legend of Gordie Howe, he currently holds 24 team records to Howe's 10. Of the Red Wings' career leaders in goals and points, Yzerman trails only Howe. But Yzerman's quiet, steady demeanor on and off the ice more closely resembles the man he just passed on those lists, Alex Delvecchio.

Like Delvecchio, Yzerman strives to produce more assists than goals, he leads by example and he's beloved by teammates and fans. Like Delvecchio, Yzerman doesn't draw attention to his prowess, and consequently doesn't always receive the recognition he deserves.

Despite being woefully underappreciated by coaches like Mike Keenan, Bryan Murray and Scotty Bowman, despite facing serious injuries to his collarbone, his right knee and his back, despite suffering painful setbacks in the playoffs almost every year of the past decade, Steve Yzerman has never quit working, never quit respecting the press or fans, and never quit fighting for Detroit's first Stanley Cup since 1955.

As a result, Detroit fans have never quit cheering for their favorite player, Steve Yzerman.

Late start, quick rise

The Norris family ended its 50-year ownership of the Detroit Red Wings when they sold the franchise to pizza baron Mike Ilitch on June 22, 1982. By any standard, the organization was a shambles. The once-proud Red Wings employed 13 head coaches during the previous 13 seasons, missing the playoffs in all but two of those campaigns.

To get the Red Wings flying again, Ilitch and then-general manager Jim Devellano knew they had to use their first pick in the 1983 draft to sign a player strong enough to build a franchise around.

One possibility was a quiet, unassuming junior player who had just turned 18. He was a relatively small at 5-foot-11, 170 pounds; his numbers with the Peterborough Petes of the Ontario Hockey League were solid, but not staggering; and he had only started playing hockey 10 years earlier.

But something about the kid felt right.

Steve Yzerman was born May 9, 1965, in Cranbrook, British Columbia. He spent the first nine years of his life there until his father, Ron Yzerman, who worked for the Canadian government's health and welfare department, moved the family to Napean, Ontario, a suburb of Ottawa.

Young Yzerman had only picked up the game that would forever change his life two years ear-

Career vs. NHL

How Yzerman has fared against NHL teams:

Team	GP	G	A	Pts.
Anaheim	11	8	8	16
Boston	30	19	19	38
Buffalo	32	22	34	56
Calgary	41	21	19	40
Chicago	92	42	70	112
Colorado	33	20	24	44
Dallas	87	39	77	116
Edmonton	37	34	27	61
Florida	4	2	6	8
Hartford	29	11	21	32
Los Angeles	40	25	33	58
Montreal	30	16	21	37
New Jersey	31	10	30	40
NY Islanders	28	15	21	36
NY Rangers	29	16	20	36
Ottawa	5	2	2	4
Philadelphia	32	25	27	52
Pittsburgh	31	14	27	41
San Jose	17	6	14	20
St. Louis	88	39	63	102
Tampa Bay	12	12	15	27
Toronto	88	56	76	132
Vancouver	40	25	27	52
Washington	32	15	27	42
Winnipeg	43	23	30	53

lier, at age 7 — a very late start by hockey standards; players like Wayne Gretzky began the sport on backyard ponds at age 2 or 3. Unlike other sports that come intuitively, hockey players must master three foreign elements — skates, stick and ice — before becoming creative playmakers.

Steve Yzerman unleashes a slap shot against Chicago in the 1989 playoffs.

Steve Yzerman was a fast study. Ten years after playing his first organized game, he was playing in the NHL. Steve Yzerman has played 30 percent longer in the NHL than all other levels combined.

"It's all I ever wanted to do," he said.

Yzerman was picked fourth overall in the 1983 draft, behind Brian Lawton, Sylvain Turgeon and Pat LaFontaine. Of the top 10 picks that year, only one other player, New Jersey's John MacLean, is still playing with his original team, and no one from that draft has come close

to Yzerman's production.

"We wanted one player which we could build a team around," Devellano said. "From Day 1, Steve Yzerman has been our bright hope. As best as you can know a 17-year-old, we felt we had found our cornerstone. We started out together."

Devellano's first decision might have been his best one.

Roller coaster

Yzerman vindicated Devellano's decision his first night in uniform, Oct. 5, 1983, when he had a goal and an assist against Winnipeg. He kept it up the entire season, becoming the youngest representative at the NHL All-Star Game, finishing second to goalie Tom Barrasso

Career Statistics

Season	Club	League	Regular Schedule					Playoffs				
			GP	G	A	P	PM	GP	G	A	P	PM
1981-82	Peterborough	OHL	58	21	43	64	65	6	0	1	1	16
1982-83	Peterborough	OHL	56	42	49	91	33	4	1	4	5	0
1983-84	Detroit	NHL	80	39	48	87	33	4	3	3	6	0
1984-85	Detroit	NHL	80	30	59	89	58	3	2	1	3	2
1985-86	Detroit	NHL	51	14	28	42	16	-	-	-	-	-
1986-87	Detroit	NHL	80	31	59	90	43	16	5	13	18	8
1987-88	Detroit	NHL	64	50	52	102	44	3	1	3	4	6
1988-89	Detroit	NHL	80	65	90	155	61	6	5	5	10	2
1989-90	Detroit	NHL	79	62	65	127	79	-	-	-	-	-
1990-91	Detroit	NHL	80	51	57	108	34	7	3	3	6	4
1991-92	Detroit	NHL	79	45	58	103	64	11	3	5	8	12
1992-93	Detroit	NHL	84	58	79	137	44	7	4	3	7	4
1993-94	Detroit	NHL	58	24	58	82	36	3	1	3	4	0
1995	Detroit	NHL	47	12	26	38	40	15	4	8	12	0
1995-96	Detroit	NHL	80	36	59	95	64	18	8	12	20	4
TOTALS			942	517	738	1255	616	93	39	59	98	42

for Rookie of the Year honors, setting Red Wings rookie records for goals and leading the team in points. That summer he became the youngest member of Team Canada in the Canada Cup — a team that would snub him later in his career.

Yzerman had 87 and 89 points in his first two seasons, helping his team make the playoffs in consecutive years for the first time since 1966 — when Delvecchio was captain.

Season of discontent

As is so often the case with Yzerman, right when things look rosiest, Job-like circumstances seem to conspire to tangle his good works. The seeds for the Red Wings' demise were sown in the spring of 1988, when Petr Klima, Bob Probert and other players were caught breaking curfew before their second consecutive conference finals matchup with the Oilers.

Red Wings coach Jacques Demers, who had taken the coaching reigns in 1986, went against conventional coaching wisdom by excusing the players because they were so important to the team's success, which eventually undermined the value system by which all teams must function: Namely, no player is above the rules. Demers began to lose control of his team thereafter.

Probert's personal battle with alcohol and drug addictions only worsened afterward, until finally he was caught with cocaine hidden in his pants when trying to cross the U.S. border from Windsor. By Oct. 26, 1989, Probert faced a deportation hearing on importing cocaine into the U.S., which eventually resulted in his not being allowed to travel with the Red Wings to Canada.

Despite all the problems, in the fall of 1989 the Red Wings still looked like a team on the rise. Demers' welcome, however, began to wear thin. Demers is generally credited in hockey circles for his ability to motivate underachieving teams to great success for a few years, but he is not a tactician, and has lacked staying power at every one of his NHL stops.

Yzerman did all he could, with 62 goals and 65 assists for 127 points, but it was far from enough. The Red Wings went from first to worst in their division during the 1989-90 season, missing the playoffs for the first time since Demers became coach three years earlier.

At the end of the season, Demers stepped down as head coach shortly after season's end.

In the process, Yzerman lost perhaps his biggest fan. Demers relied heavily on Yzerman, often consulting with his captain on decisions great and small, and doting on his prize player with a father's pride. Even when he was coaching the Stanley Cup champion Canadiens years later, Demers said, "I can honestly say he is the greatest player I've ever coached."

Although some felt his charm wore off near the end of his stay in Detroit, Demers' charisma was undeniable. His replacement, Bryan Murray, had all the sparkle of a glass of skim milk, without the flavor.

Yzerman continued his solid play during his

Yzerman struggles to open a bottle of champagne for his new bride, Lisa, in 1989.

first year under Murray, getting more than 50 goals and 100 points for the fourth consecutive year. Nonetheless, when the 1990-91 season ended and the Red Wings had quickly fallen by the wayside in the playoffs again, it marked the third straight year the team failed to return to the conference finals. For the first time in his seven-year career, trade rumors included Yzerman's name.

Adding insult to injury, Yzerman's reputation for hard, intelligent play was going unappreciated by national team coaches. Mike Keenan, then coach of the Chicago Blackhawks, also coached Team Canada in the Canada Cup series in 1987 and 1991. Despite making the team in 1984 and playing much better hockey since, Yzerman was cut by Keenan in 1987, universally shocking hockey observers.

In the 1990 World Championships in Switzerland, Yzerman led all Team Canada players with nine goals and 10 assists. Keenan subsequently promised him a spot on the 1991 Canada Cup team before tryouts began.

But Keenan has a history of changing his mind. Despite his promise, Keenan cut Yzerman again in 1991. Keenan blamed the decision on Yzerman's poor training-camp performance, although Yzerman pointed out that Mark Messier skipped the entire pretournament preparation, yet was still named a starter on the team the day he showed up. Messier making the team ahead of him, that Yzerman could accept. But when lesser lights like Dirk Graham, Brent Sutter and Steve Larmer made the team, Yzerman had to shake his head. Oh, and 18-year-old Eric Lindros, who had yet to play a game in the NHL, also made the squad.

"I know inside it's killing him," Demers said of Keenan's slighting Yzerman. "I feel for him. This ... has to hurt."

Yzerman maintained his usual brave front. "No, it doesn't hurt all that much," Yzerman said. "A little, maybe, but all in a day's work."

Still, it was obvious some of Yzerman's youthful faith in others had been lost.

"I've always been concerned with what everybody thinks," he said. "I've tried to say the right things in public, say the right things to the coaches. (But) you kind of realize that you can't always take people's words as true. The game

Yzerman at Oak Park Arena in his first practice following a knee injury in 1985.

is a business. I understand that (now).

"You can't think people are going to take care of you because you're a good guy."

A new attitude

From the ashes of the Red Wings' latest implosion, management built the current unit. Darren McCarty, Kris Draper and the Russian Revolution all came on board while the Red Wings went through another rebuilding process. There have been so many changes the past five years that Yzerman, the former wunderkind, was now the senior statesman. No other player had played for the Red Wings half as many seasons as he had. Of the 13 first-round picks Detroit had selected since Yzerman, only Martin Lapointe is currently on the team.

Since Yzerman joined the Red Wings in 1983, Detroit had hired seven different coaches, and had made 82 transactions involving more than 100 players.

With the new flood of talented teammates, Yzerman has had to make sacrifices. After making the All-Star team for six consecutive years and being the Red Wings' points leader for eight straight seasons, Yzerman hasn't accomplished either feat in three years. Since players like Sergei Fedorov and Vyacheslav Kozlov can pick up more of the

The Red Wings bench during Game 3 of the 1991 playoffs against St. Louis.

scoring load, Yzerman has re-emphasized team defense, and no longer plays the 35-minute games he used to under Demers.

The irony is a bit cruel: Yzerman might have won the 1988 MVP award if he had played on a bona fide Cup contender; now that he's final-

ly playing for one, he's no longer the premier player. That's how Fedorov won the Hart Trophy in 1993-94.

Nonetheless, Murray's final season and Scotty Bowman's first offered more bitter pills to swallow. In 1992-93 and 1993-94, the Red

Wings broke the 100-point plateau in the regular season, only to get wiped out in the first round of the playoffs. Adding to Yzerman's loss, his best friend, Gerard Gallant, left in the summer of 1994.

That season, the Red Wings' captain also suffered a herniated disc in his back, and endured more trade rumors. "If it's time to go, it's time to go," he said. "I just wish I would be treated with a little more respect."

If the respect from the front office was underwhelming, the chorus of respect from the fans was unmistakable. As the rumors again circulated in the fall of 1995 during a long road trip, upon his return to Joe Louis the crowd gave Yzerman a rousing ovation when his name was announced before the game. Bowman was probably smart enough to calculate how unpopular he would be in this town if he traded Yzerman.

Yzerman has other consolations to savor these days. In 1993, the management renegotiated his contract a second time, this one for about $13 million over four seasons. The same year, his wife Lisa gave birth to Isabella, their first child.

Whether it's because Yzerman knows he has a happy home life to support him, or conversely that he realizes a sudden injury or unexpected trade could end his tenure in Detroit tomorrow, Yzerman seems to be enjoying the game more than ever.

A good example is his 500th career goal, which he scored on a backhand shot past Patrick Roy in a 3-2 victory over Colorado on Jan. 16, 1996. The Red Wings' bench emptied and Chris Osgood skated into Colorado territory to celebrate with their captain while the crowd gave him a two-minute ovation.

"I've never seen that smile before," Ciccarelli said. "He's such a serious guy, such a hard worker. He'd (normally) blow it off like it was no big deal, but that smile was different."

"All I feel is simply happiness," Yzerman said. "I used to take this game so seriously. Now I enjoy it, I'm looser.

"The part that pleases me the most is that I've been here for 13 years to get them. I see faces in the crowd I've recognized for 13 years, people I've met there, people who work in the building. They've seen my whole career. They shared in this."

Yzerman's fans

It is the night of April 12, 1996. It's been a big night for Steve Yzerman. The NHL presented him with a gift for his 500th goal before the game, his team went on to win its record 61st contest, and his parents had flown in from Ottawa to see it all with his wife and daughter.

Yzerman is one of the first players to emerge from the locker room near midnight. Everyone hugs each other, talks a bit, then starts walking down the hallway that circles Joe Louis Arena under the stands. It's a huge corridor, easily 25 feet across, and usually quiet after games. But when Yzerman walks down it, people you would never notice along the walls spring to life, like toys in the *Nutcracker Suite*.

Two girls in Red Wings jerseys scream, "Stevie! Stevie!" He stops and he signs their jerseys, then catches up with his family.

Seeing this, a middle-aged guy wearing a mustache, a curly mop of black hair and an open collared shirt spreads his arms wide in protest, and yells at Yzerman from 20 paces like they're

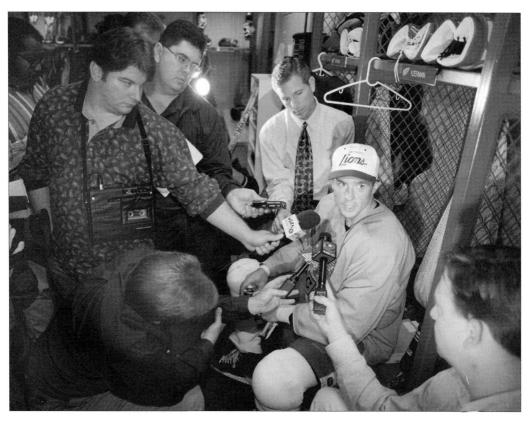

Yzerman, at his locker after practice in 1995, responds to questions from the media.

both in the mob.

"Heeeeey! Steeeevie! Come ON! You never did it for us laaaast time!" Everything about this guy screams: keep moving. But Yzerman waits for the guy, and signs without a peep. He trots to catch up to his family but he doesn't get far: The scene is repeated a dozen times while Yzerman tries to keep moving.

By now, he is in a full-fledged sprint between signings. Just when he thinks he's free, an elderly woman he doesn't know catches him at the door and says, "Ohhh, Steeevie, give me a hug." She holds his arm, looks into his eyes and asks

about his parents and family — all of whom are waiting for her to let him go.

Yzerman is kind and patient, while sneaking glances with his family on the other side of the door. They've waited 15 minutes for him to walk a few hundred yards.

Finally, they're all in his car, and drive up to the parking lot exit. A thirtysomething woman who sells the players' autographs at shows yells, "That's Yzerman! STEVIE, STEVIE!" But he drives through.

"That's Yzerman," she says to no one, "He never signs."

"The guys who are selling them, they've

Yzerman scores against the Mighty Ducks in 1995.

already got 'em all," Yzerman says. "I try to make a point of getting the mother and the father in the back of the crowd with the little girl."

It's no small task. The vendors that separate the Yzerman from the true fans have a lot more experience, and a stronger motive: money.

The players' hastily-inked wiggles now constitute a multibillion-dollar industry. Yzerman's and Fedorov's usually go for about $50. A signed jersey by Yzerman can get $250 at a charity auction.

Yzerman's former teammate, Mike Ramsey, said "The shame of it is, a few people ruin it for the majority of people for whom it means something — and I don't even get bugged half as much as Yzerman."

When Steve Yzerman was once signing at the Detroit Boat Show, a vendor off to the side was giving three Red Wings pucks to each empty-handed kid for Yzerman to sign, provided they

returned two to him. The kids got what they wanted, the vendor got what he wanted — and Yzerman's work tripled.

Just the same, Yzerman would rather get burned once in a while by a vendor than risk losing contact with the real fans.

Mike Ramsey recalled a scene from his final season in the NHL — with the Red Wings: "We were all on the bus in Chicago when I saw Yzerman trying to get on with two bags on his shoulders, and they're all jamming paper in his face. But just as he's about to get on, he sees a little girl in the crowd with a Red Wings jersey on, so he stops to sign it. That's when it means something."

Of course, the vendors around her were outraged — how can she get one and not them? — but the little girl ran off into the night, hugging her signature.

One person, at least, went home happy that night.

The last details

Yzerman's career lacks just one thing: It's big and silver and great for drinking victory champagne from. To sip from it, Yzerman is beginning to challenge his teammates in ways he never would earlier in his captaincy.

The 1995 Stanley Cup playoffs seemed like the time. The Red Wings buzzed through the first three rounds, only to be swept by the upstart New Jersey Devils in four games.

After winning a league-record 62 regular-season games in 1995-96, everyone picked the Red Wings as the Cup favorites, but they were soon on the ropes against St. Louis. When Detroit lost Game 5 to the Blues to trail three games to two, Yzerman guaranteed the Red Wings would win Game 6.

"He's brought his determination and leadership to another level," Ciccarelli said. "It's really rubbing off on the other guys. You couldn't write a better script."

Just 1:15 into the second overtime of Game 7, Yzerman took matters into his own hands by burying the Gretzky-led Blues. His goal sent his team to the conference finals for the fourth time in 10 years.

"If anything, our will has gotten stronger, our confidence has grown," he said.

But that's not much for the hottest playoff goalie in the game. Roy and the Avalanche put the clamps on the Red Wings, setting them back with a 3-1 lead in games.

"I know we need our top players to step up and assert themselves on the ice, in the locker room and with the media," Yzerman said, flexing his newfound provocative style. "It's time for the guys with the age and experience to assert themselves."

When asked if he was referring to Fedorov and Keith Primeau, Yzerman simply said, "Yes."

Yzerman's cajoling wasn't enough, of course. Detroit showed some grit, but ultimately lost, 4-2, in games to the eventual Stanley Cup champions. As a result, he must continue listening to comments like the one Montreal General Manager Serge Savard uttered two years ago. When he signed Patrick Roy for $4 million per year, he justified it by saying that Roy had won Stanley Cups, whereas "a guy like Yzerman has never won anything." It was a low blow, one Yzerman characteristically brushed off with little comment.

Yzerman can afford to let it pass since he and his team have plenty of life left. Last season, Yzerman scored the team's first goal 10 times and the lead goal 16 times, more often than any other Red Wing. In other words, Yzerman still gets the Red Wings started and still puts them over the top.

He finished the season second on the team in goals, third in assists, and its leader in points-per-game.

His team also is very much in the hunt. Since Yzerman joined the Red Wings in 1983, they have finished at least third in their division 11 times in the past 13 years, and in first place six times.

But there is that last, unfinished detail that Yzerman knows his career will be incomplete without.

"I sit and watch every year as the Stanley Cup is being presented to someone else," he said. "I talk to guys who have won it. I realize what it means."

Chapter Two

The Quiet Leader

By Cynthia Lambert

Martin Lapointe sat in front of his dressing room stall and smiled as he stared across the room. A scene from the 1996 NHL playoffs was replaying in his mind.

It was memorable mostly because Lapointe didn't see it happen often. Like a snowstorm in May or a failing grade for an honor student, the uniqueness of the event made it a time that stood out from the others.

"I'll never forget when Steve stood up in the room during the playoffs last year," Lapointe said, rubbing his chin. "It was against Colorado. He told us what we needed to do. He's so well-respected. Every time he talks, people shut it down and listen. And the thing with Steve is that he doesn't use any extra words."

Steve Yzerman has gone through many changes during his long career in Detroit. The once shy and reserved center emerged not only as the Red Wings' leader, but he is known around the league — and beyond — as a role model for integrity and leading by example, often silently.

"In order to be a leader, you have to have players who want to be led," forward Doug

Brown said. "I think with the team we've had recently, Steve has players who want to be led, which helps him do his job."

Yzerman's role has expanded, but its primary function is on the ice.

"He's an unbelievable example on the ice," said Igor Larionov, a player who has been known for his steady leadership and talent both in Russia and in the NHL. "He gives his best effort every night. Steve Yzerman is the heart of this Red Wings team. He leads by example and I think that is the best way to do it. The best talk is when you score some nice goals and show the team the way."

But Yzerman, in his never-ending quest to win the Stanley Cup, has had to do more than lead by example. There are times when actions must be supported or punctuated by words.

"I feel more comfortable in that situation than I did five or six years ago," said Yzerman, the Red Wings' captain for the past 11 years. "I do feel comfortable talking with the group we have now. Maybe it's because I'm older now. I think age has something to do with it.

"I'm not a big believer in standing up and

Red Wings coach Jacques Demers names Yzerman team captain in 1986.

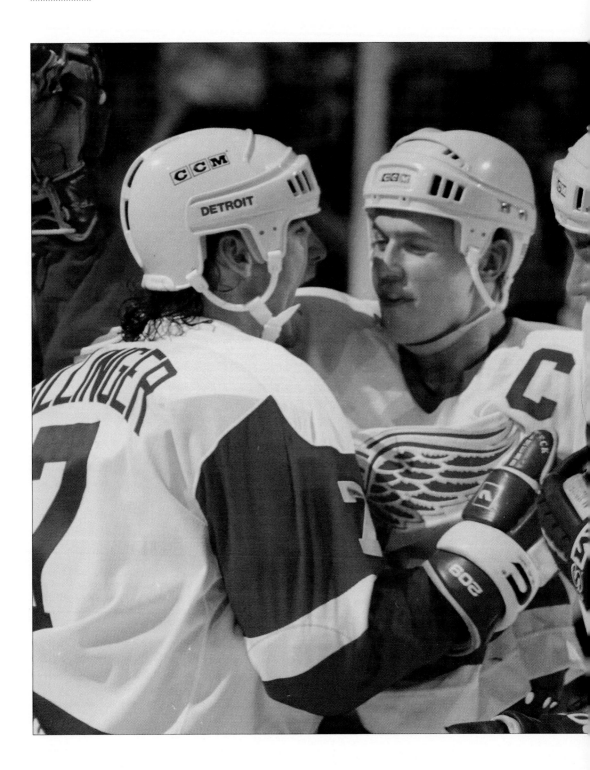

(Left to right) Mike Sillinger, Yzerman, Keith Primeau and Brad McCrimmon celebrate a playoff goal against St. Louis in 1991.

giving a big speech. I think it's overrated. I think it's for the movies. It's easier to stand up and say something in front of a group of people than to pull someone aside and say something to them. That's what's most difficult to do."

During the 1996 Western Conference finals against the Avalanche, it was Yzerman who addressed the media before the third and fourth games. As he was questioned about Detroit's ineffectiveness against Colorado, Yzerman answered with a candidness no other player in the dressing room could or would offer.

In that same press conference, Yzerman said his teammates had to be more responsible for leading the team not only on the ice, but on the bench, in the dressing room and with the media. In the end, only a handful of players responded and the Wings lost the series in six games.

Despite the exit, Yzerman didn't lose his hope, didn't blame or point fingers. Instead, he spent time talking about his insatiable thirst to win it all.

"I never lose hope," Yzerman said, eyes wide, showing the sincerity of his words. "I'm always ready to start another season."

In the 1996 playoffs, Yzerman led the team with eight goals and 12 assists for 20 points in 18 games. His most significant goal was the biggest one for the team, the one that kept them in the postseason.

"To look at Steve's leadership ability I think you only have to look at the goal he scored against St. Louis in the second round, Game 7," said Red Wings assistant coach Dave Lewis, who also played with Yzerman from 1986-88. "It was double-overtime and he got the winner. That is leadership to me. Isn't it funny how the guys who usually score those big goals are considered their team's leader.

"No, to me, you don't have to look any further than that goal against St. Louis to show just what a good leader Steve is."

Yzerman agreed that any team's leader has to be counted on to do the right thing at the right time. It's a responsibility he accepted from the day he was drafted by the Red Wings.

"There is truth in that, not so much as scoring the big goals, but I do believe the guys who are the best leaders are the ones who make things happen," Yzerman said. "Leaders have to take charge, they have to assert themselves."

But Yzerman didn't arrive in Detroit as a leader. He was a fresh-faced, wide-eyed 18-year-old who spoke only when spoken to. Beyond that, he was in poor shape physically.

Yzerman's conditioning was so poor it prompted former trainer Jim Pengelly to tell then-coach Nick Polano that, according to the strength testing done, Yzerman would not be able to compete in the NHL.

"I remember telling him, 'This is our first-round pick. If he can't play, we're in real trouble,' " Polano recalled.

"But at the first scrimmage during that training camp, I remember seeing Steve take the puck, beat (defenseman) John Barrett, shuffle Greg Stefan out of the net and put the puck in the top right-hand corner — a move only a real pro can make. I looked at Jim and said, 'That's that Yzerman guy you said would never play.' "

Obviously, Yzerman's conditioning habits have changed dramatically over the years. It's yet another way he leads by example.

Yzerman's combination of talent and leader-

Red Wings great Sid Abel visits with Yzerman at Joe Louis Arena in 1986.

ship is just what the floundering Red Wings needed at the time. When the Red Wings made Yzerman their top selection (fourth overall) in the 1983 entry draft, it was done with great purpose and dire need. And, according to Jim Devellano, the general manager at the time, with a huge dose of luck.

"Steve played for Peterborough (OHL) and his coach was Dick Todd," Devellano said. "The way Dick ran the team was to play four lines, which meant Steve didn't get as much ice time as some of the other top prospects got with their teams. I think because of that, Steve fell to fourth and we were able to take him.

"Did we know about his leadership capabilities? Not really. What we knew was that he was a good kid and a talented player. I remember at that first training camp, within five minutes, he was the best player on the ice. That was good and bad because he was only 18 years old, was 5-11 and probably didn't even weigh 160 pounds.

"We were very high on Steve and we knew it was important to start the rebuilding process

**Yzerman reflects on a playoff loss to
St. Louis in 1986.**

with the team."

What the Red Wings needed was a player to hang their hopes on, and Yzerman proved to be that foundation.

Mike Ilitch had purchased the club the summer before and had seen his new project finish out of the playoffs, with a 21-44-15 record under Polano. Yzerman was determined not only to improve the club's record, but to put fans in the empty seats at Joe Louis Arena. The young star had enough fortitude to accomplish the former, and enough dazzle to provide the latter.

"It's different to look at kids who are so young, like Steve was when he came to the Wings, and think of leadership," said former defenseman Colin Campbell, who played in Detroit during Yzerman's first two seasons. "Steve was awfully young. I think his first year you might have looked more at (second-round pick) Lane Lambert as the leader because he was more aggressive. Ten years later Lane disappeared, but Steve certainly didn't.

"I think it's typical to look at players who are boisterous and vociferous and say they smack of leadership. That's not always the case. Steve isn't either of those.

"Steve has been a unique and good person for the franchise. He is the beacon that keeps on shining. That is a great definition of a leader."

In Yzerman's first year the Red Wings improved 12 points, led by Yzerman's 39 goals while playing on a line with John Ogrodnick and Ron Duguay. Ogrodnick remembers the 1983 version of Yzerman as do most. And like many, Ogrodnick saw a spark of leadership.

"As an 18-year-old coming into the league, Steve was shy, real shy," Ogrodnick said. "Some-

Yzerman, horsing around during a practice session in 1996.

times you see guys with the talent he had come into the league cocky and outspoken. Steve wasn't like that.

"You could tell right away he was a very talented player. When a guy is that talented, unless he's obnoxious, he's going to be a leader to some degree. With Steve it was a combination of his talent on the ice and his personality off it that worked."

That combination is what prompted Polano to first consider Yzerman as the captain of the Red Wings. It was the spring of 1985, and Yzerman was playing for Team Canada in the World Championships in Prague, Czechoslovakia.

"I went to the World Championships that year," Polano said. "I remember we went out for dinner in Prague. I told Steve then that if I returned as coach the next year I would have him as my captain. I said, 'You're ready now.' I watched him for two years and saw him leading in a quiet manner."

Yzerman recalled that dinner with Polano with a smile and with memories.

"I remember it, sure," Yzerman said. "I remember I was a bit surprised by it. I don't even know if I had turned 20 yet and he was talking to me about being the captain.

"In minor hockey all of the guys who are here (in the NHL) were the top players so we were all captains or assistants. But in minor hockey you just wore it on your jersey. You didn't really do anything other than go to get the trophy at the tournament."

Considering the state of the Red Wings when Yzerman arrived, he had to quickly hone his leadership abilities. It is also when he started his reputation as one who leads through example.

"A good leader is a guy who's self-motivated, a guy a coach doesn't have to work on every day," Polano said. "Steve practiced hard, he played hard. I've found that usually guys who practice hard are your best players. This was a guy who worked extra all the time. The coach needs someone in that locker room who can almost be another assistant coach. I know Mark Messier does it and I thought Steve could do it."

Yzerman had just turned 20 when Polano asked him if he would accept the captaincy. Yzerman's youth was not a factor to him. But Polano didn't return as coach the following season. Instead, he was replaced by Harry Neale, who was then replaced by Brad Park midway

Minnesota goalie Jon Casey towers over Yzerman after stopping a goal-scoring chance in 1992.

through the season.

The following year, the 1986-87 season, Jacques Demers took over as coach. During that training camp, Demers announced that Yzerman would be the team's captain. It was a move questioned by some, considering Yzerman's age. He was just 21. But Demers followed through with his wish to have Yzerman ordained as the Red Wings' official leader.

And at the start of the 1986-87 season, a year after the team set a franchise low for points (40), Yzerman, then 21, was named the youngest captain in the long history of the organization. It would be his job to lead his team out of the darkness of disappointment, out of the monotony of mediocrity.

"I was at the draft after I was named coach in the summer of 1986," Demers said. "And I met Steve Yzerman there in Montreal. I talked with him, and he told me that he could not accept that his team finished with 40 points the year before and that he wasn't having a good summer because of it. That a young guy like him could live with that disappointment in that way, where he simply would not accept it, that showed me something. He showed me that he cared so much about the team.

"He knew what people were saying about the Wings, saying they were the Dead Wings. They were the laughing stock of the league and that hurt him. He was so embarrassed. I knew then that this guy could be the leader of the team, the captain. He had to be."

So the Yzerman era began in earnest.

But before Yzerman could progress as a captain, he had to figure out how to be a captain. It wasn't an easy assignment for the next cou-

Yzerman wipes out the Vancouver goalie during the first period of a 1992 contest.

ple of years, particularly since the Red Wings' dressing room was filled with older, more established players such as Glen Hanlon, Harold Snepsts, Tim Higgins and Lewis.

Yzerman views those days as being more of a figure head than an actual active captain.

"Basically, I was the captain, but those other guys were the team leaders," Yzerman said. "They were all 31 or 32ish. They were married and had families. There wasn't much I could tell them. There really wasn't a whole lot I could say to them."

So Yzerman worked on the ice, leading through

the conference finals against Edmonton, a mete-oric rise from the cellar.

"He was awesome," Demers said. "He led them as well as any person ever. It was in the way he played — hard and with intensity. He got a lot of points because he played so hard. Back then he was the only star we had, no question. And there were nights, if not weeks, when Steve Yzerman carried the Detroit Red Wings on his shoulders.

"I believe his leadership came from a determination," Demers said. "He worked his butt off and he took pride in what the team did. What I found in Steve Yzerman was his desire to win every night. I don't ever remember a night when Steve Yzerman did not come to play. He would

score the clutch goals.

"I knew this man would not accept losing. I know we had a number of players who came up big in games, guys like Glen Hanlon, Harold Snepsts, Bob Probert and Joe Kocur, Shawn Burr. But you have to have that one guy who will be there all of the time. Steve Yzerman was that for the Detroit Red Wings. Chicago has that with Michael Jordan and San Francisco had it with Joe Montana. The one guy who would make a difference for us was Steve Yzerman. You could count on it."

Nearly a decade later, in the fall of 1995, Yzerman's effectiveness was being questioned. Scotty Bowman, the coach and director of player personnel, began talks with the Ottawa Sena-

Red Wings fans celebrate Yzerman and the team's victory over Chicago — their 61st regular season win in 1996.

tors regarding Yzerman. News of the conversations leaked to the media.

What resulted was a major revolt by fans in Detroit, and even among some in the Red Wings' organization. On opening night, when Yzerman was introduced at Joe Louis Arena, the fans gave their vote with a chilling standing ovation. It was a message — loud and clear — to the hierarchy attempting a change of venue for the only captain some Red Wings fans ever knew.

Today, Yzerman views the situation optimistically.

"It was good," he said, allowing a smile as he thought back to craziness of the plight. "Not necessarily the part about maybe getting traded, but going through a situation like that. It keeps you kind of humble. It allows you to go through a situation that a majority of players do go through. After going through something like that, you can relate a little bit better to the guys."

Until Yzerman's name surfaced in the trade rumors, he was associated with Detroit much like the Tigers' Alan Trammell or the Lions' Barry Sanders.

"You can go your entire career and have things go your way," Yzerman said. "But the reality is, players are traded, they play in the minors, they're sat out. Some of those experiences are good to go through because they help you learn to deal with them, you learn how to deal with adversity."

And some of Yzerman's fondest memories are of how his teammates rallied around him while the trade rumors swirled. It wasn't that they did support their captain, it was *how*. Despite his prominence in the Detroit sports scene for more than a decade and his certain future Hall of Fame

stature, Yzerman was treated as though he were just one of the guys. For him, it was as high a compliment as any of his teammates could pay him.

"Throughout that first month we had a lot of fun with it," Yzerman said. "In the locker room there was a lot of ribbing. We had a lot of laughs with the whole thing. I wasn't thrilled about being in the situation of being mentioned in a trade, but when guys in the room are firing shots at one another, it's nice to be a part of it. I knew then that everyone in our room was fair game. And I enjoyed hearing a 21- or 22-year-old kid going after me. It helped the atmosphere."

A captain, a true leader, can recognize such things.

Chapter Three

The Passing of the Torch

By Vartan Kupelian
....

Every great team has a signature star. It is a truism in every sport, at every level.

There never has been a dynasty without a figurehead, a player who embodies the whole. The heart, the soul, the inspiration.

The power.

In the 1960's, a professor of classical mythology lectured a class at Wayne State University. The day's lesson was of myths and mortals, gods and their companions.

The lecturer began, "There is a man among us today who, were he living during the Golden Age of the Greeks, would be revered ... transformed from man to myth, from mortal to legend."

The professor asked: "Who is this man?"

There were a few obligatory guesses, none remotely close to solving the riddle.

The lecturer continued: "He has the strength of 10 men ... a powerful man with a thick neck and sloping shoulders. His exploits and heroism are legendary. He

Gordie Howe in 1967

has survived all enemies, arrows and spears."

Annoyed that no one could decode the clues, he finally gave in. The professor, you see, was a hockey nut and his idol was Gordie Howe.

Gordie Howe, the greatest hockey player of them all, was born in the remote outpost of Floral, Saskatchewan, on Canada's great western prairie, on March 31, 1928. It was a day so bitterly cold that the ice beneath his skates was a birthright.

Like a mythological figure, he played hockey well into his 50's and through five decades. He debuted with the Detroit Red Wings in 1946 and continued to play through the 1950's, 1960's, 1970's, and briefly in the 1980's.

When Howe retired from the Red Wings in 1971 after 25 seasons, he had done things no athlete, not even Howe himself, dreamed possible. He had played in 1,687 regular-season games, he had 786 goals and 1,023 assists for 1,809 points — all NHL records at the time. He also held the record for most penalty minutes. He won the Hart Trophy as the league's most valuable player six times, the Art Ross Trophy as leading scorer six times. He was a first-team All-Star selection 11 times — remember, this was in an era with Maurice (Rocket) Richard — and second team eight times. He held no less than 25 club records.

But, most importantly, he played on four Stanley Cup championship teams in Detroit and nine first-place teams.

After a brief retirement, he returned in 1974 to resume his career with the World Hockey Association's Houston Aeros. With the Aeros, Howe fulfilled his fondest wish by joining his sons, Marty and Mark, on the same line. At age

Yzerman was the second player to score 500 goals in a Red Wings uniform.

Gordie Howe (9) maneuvers around a New York Rangers defender at Madison Square Garden in 1959.

45, he was a first team All-Star in the WHA (and again in 1975) and played in international competition with Team Canada in Russia.

The Russians, awed by this grand old champion, called him, "The man with two hearts."

Max McNab, later a NHL general manager, was a teammate of Howe's nearly a half-century ago. Like friends and foes, he marveled at No. 9's superhuman abilities.

"Mother Nature made a big mistake with Gordie Howe," McNab once said, pausing to heighten the anticipation. "She gave him everything — and forgot some other people."

Howe was the fiercest of competitors. He had legendary strength and skill, but he also had a mean streak on the ice. Opponents cowered at the site of the powerfully-built 6-footer, whose long, smooth stride defied his locomotive-like force.

Cross Gordie Howe, and retribution would come with the vengeance of Zeus. His elbows were as lethal as lightning bolts.

Bryan Watson, among the NHL's career leaders in penalties and one of its most combative players, became a teammate and close friend of Howe's later in his career. Their introduction wasn't so friendly.

"My first game in the NHL was against the Red Wings," Watson said. "I was with the Montreal Canadiens then, and they threw me out to kill a penalty. I went into the corner with Howe, knocked him down from behind and skated away with the puck. I hadn't gone very far before I heard heavy strides coming up behind me, and I felt a stick slipping under my arm. There's the blade ... not an inch from my nose. It's Howe and he says, 'Check out, Junior.' I got so scared I fell down."

It is no wonder that Gordie Howe was christened by his teammates with the nickname Power.

Silk.

As in silky smooth.

Times change, and people do, too. Personalities change, and perceptions, too.

When Steve Yzerman broke in with the Red Wings, he quickly earned a special nickname from his teammates.

They called him Silk.

As in silky smooth.

Few call Steve Yzerman by that nickname anymore. Perhaps it's a function of age. He's still smooth after all these years, but he's an adult now and his role has changed. He's no longer just a slick kid admired by other youngsters. He's the leader, the captain, and the distinction deserves a more noble portrayal. After all, Steve Yzerman is the player who will lead the Red

Wings back to the future, back to the glory days. Back to the Stanley Cup.

It's been that way since he was drafted by the Red Wings in the first round (fourth overall) in 1983. They said he would be the foundation — the first block in the bridge to glory.

"He is the cornerstone," General Manager Jimmy Devellano, who made the selection, proclaimed that day.

It was the first draft for Devellano as boss of the Red Wings and Yzerman held a special spot in the order of things. He was the first No. 1 of the Mike Ilitch era. That made Yzerman special. He always would be special. And, from the first day he skated in a winged-wheel Detroit jersey, Yzerman proved it.

"We wanted one player around which we could build a team," Devellano said. "From Day 1, Steve Yzerman has been our bright hope."

As an 18-year-old rookie, Yzerman did everything that could be expected of a teen-ager. He became the youngest to play in the NHL All-Star Game. But he was still a baby. Quiet, reserved, not yet the leader he would be one day. He still had to find his way around the NHL.

The Red Wings, with Yzerman centering the No. 1 line with John Ogrodnick and Ron Duguay, made the playoffs after Yzerman's first two seasons, but were eliminated in the first round. Still, it represented an improvement. Yzerman scored 87 points as a rookie, 89 in his sophomore season. The important thing was that the Red Wings, the once-proud franchise of Howe, Sid Abel, Ted Lindsay, Alex Delvecchio and a host of other Hall of Famers, had finally returned to the playoffs.

The third year of the Yzerman era was the

Comparing Greats

Comparing the career Red Wings statistics of Gordie Howe, the Wings' most prolific player, and Steve Yzerman, the Wings' most prolific player of the last 13 seasons (Howe leads the Wings in all of the categories below except shorthanded goals):

Category	Howe	Yzerman
Seasons	25	13
Games	1,687	828
Goals	786	517
Assists	1,023	738
Points	1,809	1,255
Hat tricks	18	20

worst. He started poorly, the victim of youthful inconsistency, and went downhill from there until, on Jan. 31, 1986, he suffered a broken right collarbone and missed the rest of the season. The Wings were far out of playoff contention, and even a healthy Yzerman would not have put them there. They eventually finished with 17 victories in 80 games.

What followed was a summer of discontent for Steve Yzerman. He said he felt very ordinary about himself, his abilities and his future.

"I learned a lot," Yzerman said. "I ate a lot of crow. I signed a big contract and I was embarrassed. But I was mostly scared. I knew

if I kept playing like I was, I'd be out of hockey. I couldn't stand that."

He vowed to make it different.

The soul-searching continued into training camp, where a new coach, Jacques Demers, greeted the Red Wings. On a warm September day late in camp, Demers asked Yzerman into his office. After a brief discussion, Demers entrusted Yzerman, then 21, with the team captaincy. Yzerman, the youngest captain in club history, responded in a big way and the Red Wings flourished. Note the correlation.

But Steve Yzerman wasn't satisfied.

"When I play against those guys — the Bryan

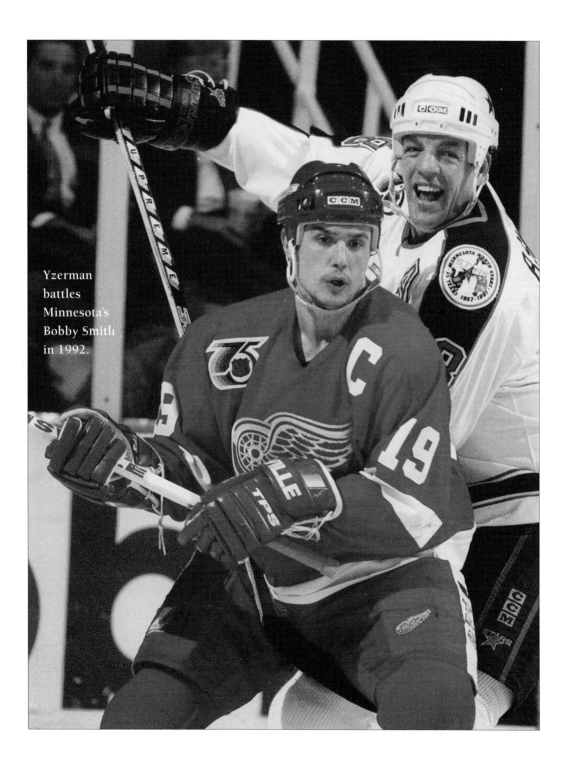

Yzerman
battles
Minnesota's
Bobby Smith
in 1992.

Trottiers, the Wayne Gretzkys, the Mark Messiers — I still feel I've got a lot to learn," Yzerman said. "There are so many little things they do so well, things they do day after day, shift after shift. I don't consider myself in that category. I feel I've made important strides but I'm still improving. Trying to, anyway."

Steve Yzerman, playing in his 14th NHL season with the Red Wings in 1996-97, has been through a lot — from the highs of the Stanley Cup Finals in 1995 to the lows of a 40-point season in 1985-86.

Yzerman began the 1996-97 season second on the Red Wings' career list in goals (517), behind Howe; third in scoring (1,255 points) and third in assists (738). Only Howe and Alex Delvecchio are ahead of him in the last two categories. He has led the team in goals and assists eight times, and in goals six times. He has surpassed the 100-point barrier six straight seasons — something 12 other players have accomplished. To top it off, he's only one of four players to score more than 150 points in a season. He did it in 1988-89. The others: Wayne Gretzky, Mario Lemieux and Phil Esposito. The best of the best.

It was in 1987-88 that Yzerman finally arrived among the NHL elite. It was time for the big boys to move over and make room at the top. On his ascension, the player his teammates called Silk smoothed the way for the Red Wings.

Power and Silk.

Two hockey players — Gordie Howe and Steve Yzerman — so different in some ways; so similar in others.

Howe, strong and menacing, a right wing who could score or smash.

Yzerman, smooth and artful, a center with dazzling moves and a surgeon's touch.

Howe always described himself as "just a lucky old farm boy."

Floral is a granary on the outskirts of Saskatoon, Saskatchewan, in Canada's wheat belt. His mother always knew Gordie, who could have excelled in other sports, would gravitate toward hockey. Howe's first skates were a hand-me-down pair so large he had to stuff newspapers in the toe to make them fit. When young Gordie came home for a meal, she would place an old newspaper on the kitchen floor so that he could keep his skates on while he ate.

Parents are like that. In another town halfway across Canada, in a west-end suburb of Ottawa, the nation's capital, Ron and Jean Yzerman also knew their investment of time, money and care in son Steve's hockey career wasn't misspent. They gladly made the sacrifices because they knew their son enjoyed the game.

"It's all I ever wanted to do," Steve Yzerman said.

The Yzermans lived in western Canada, British Columbia, when Steve, age 5, first played shinny. His father coached a team of 6-year-olds, which included son, Michael, and it wasn't long before Steve was playing above his age. Steve was 10 when the family moved east, to Nepean, and his hockey career flourished.

Steve Yzerman left home at age 16 to play junior hockey in Peterborough, Ontario, and his parents spared no effort to visit him despite the 175-mile drive.

The next stop after Peterborough: Detroit.

As a rookie at the Major-A level, Yzerman's

Referee Frank Udvari takes cover as Gordie Howe crunches a Toronto player into the boards.

reputation already had been made. Pro scouts knew all about the slick youngster who was a magician on skates. He could skate and stickhandle and shoot and, most of all, he could beat any defenseman in the league, even those several years older, one-on-one. That's the trait pro scouts always look for. If a junior couldn't beat other juniors one-on-one, he had no chance to advance to the next level. But Yzerman could beat anyone.

The draft class of '83 was vintage. Each of the top five players was labeled "can't miss." Topping the Wings' list was Sylvain Turgeon, a left wing from Quebec. Forward Brian Lawton went first overall to Minnesota and Hartford selected Turgeon. Still on the board were center Pat LaFontaine of Waterford, a Detroit suburb; Yzerman and Tom Barrasso, a high school goaltender from Massachusetts.

The New York Islanders, who had traded to move up in the draft, went with LaFontaine and the Red Wings had no interest in a goalie.

Yzerman's stock had dipped a little in his second year of Major A, through no fault of his own. A knee injury had limited his performance just enough, even though he had 42 goals and 91 points in 56 games. The Red Wings wasted little time calling his name when it was their turn.

Howe then and Yzerman now are all about talent. They share other traits, like humility and grace under pressure and an unquenchable thirst for hockey. Champions on the ice, they are gracious, unassuming and caring off the ice.

"I remember when I first came up I cut out all the newspaper pictures showing me in a Red Wing uniform just to prove that I played in the NHL," Howe said.

Yzerman's quiet, soft-spoken ways have often been misinterpreted as indifference, or a lack of leadership. It is none of those things. It is simply his personality. There is no braggadocio, no false bravado and no inflated sense of self-worth.

"For me, playing has always been more fun than being a player," Yzerman said. "Does that make sense?

"I always wanted to be here a long time and I didn't want to wear out my welcome. I didn't want people to get sick of me talking about myself all the time and I didn't want everybody to know everything about me. So I just decided a while back to live my own life and do my own thing and not get into that celebrity thing. I'm not a movie star or a rock and roll singer. I'm a hockey player, nothing to get carried away with.

"I've tried to say the right things in public, say the right things to the coaches. I have no desire to be outspoken or controversial. My style is my style. I have my own beliefs and confidence in myself."

Yzerman refuses to compromise his approach. He is what he is, a man and a player of substance, and leaves it for others to make the dis-

covery on their own. He doesn't campaign.

"Stevie doesn't try to kid anybody," said former teammate Gerard Gallant, once Yzerman's closest friend on the Red Wings. "He never goes looking for attention."

The trait has resulted in criticism of Yzerman's leadership abilities. There are no fire-and-brimstone speeches, no passionate pregame Knute Rockne-style admonitions; seldom even a raised voice.

"I think everybody watches too many movies," Yzerman said. "You see guys like John Wayne making speeches and that's not the way it is. Guys don't want to hear speeches. You work hard in practice, you play hard, you present the right image off the ice — that's my idea of leadership."

Wayne Gretzky never ranted or raved when he was leading the Edmonton Oilers to four Stanley Cup championships in five years in the mid-1980's. Paul Coffey, a star NHL defenseman, played on those Edmonton teams and he played with Yzerman for 3½ seasons in Detroit.

"Steve leads the same way Gretzky leads," Coffey said. "They're the type of guys who don't speak just to be heard. Steve expends so much energy on the ice, he can't be in here screaming after every game."

Call it an inherent goodness. Demers, the former Red Wings coach, identified that quality in Yzerman late in the 1986-87 season. Demers, a passionate French-Canadian who wears his heart on his sleeve, knew instantly what it meant and he spoke about it without fear of tempting the fates.

"It was the seventh game of the playoff series with Toronto," Demers said. "A very emotional game. We were at home and it was a very real

Yzerman hoists the Campbell Cup after the Red Wings defeated Chicago in the 1995 playoffs.

chance for a young kid to crack. But Stevie was awesome. He dominated. He led. We dominated. And, right then, this thought came to me: 'We can win the Stanley Cup someday with this man.' He'll come through for us. He really will."

Yzerman and Howe savor everything about the game, not just the games. The practices, the travel, the camaraderie, the joy, and even the despair. Both great players had to overcome serious injuries to resume their careers. For any other player, the risk and the pain would have been too great a price to pay. But it is part of the uniqueness shared by Yzerman and Howe.

Yzerman's career was threatened in March 1988, when he ripped up a knee after crashing into a goalpost. He was back for the playoffs a few weeks later.

The following season was Yzerman's best, with 155 points.

"I would never have anticipated him coming back and playing the way he has," said Devellano, the general manager. "It's a credit to his determination to get better."

Yzerman's second major medical problem was a neck injury that kept him out of 26 games in the 1993-94 season.

"When I hurt my knee the first time, I came back and played. It was no big deal," Yzerman said. "But after I hurt my neck, it made me think. You know, when you're younger you think you're immortal. Nothing can slow you down. Injuries are part of the game. Sure, there are some days you don't feel like you can last. But there are other days, the days when you feel like you can

Olympia Stadium, home to seven Red Wings Stanley Cup champions.

play until you're 50."

One did play until he was 50, and beyond. Only one. The incomparable Gordie Howe.

It was in the 1949-50 season that Howe's career was almost ended by an incident in a play-off game against Toronto. Howe, 21, underwent emergency surgery to relieve pressure on the brain that resulted from a collision with the Leafs' Ted Kennedy. Sid Abel, the center on the Wings' famed Production Line — Lindsay, Howe and Abel — was there when it happened.

"It was touch-and-go for two days," said Abel, who later coached Howe and the Red Wings. "They called in a specialist and he had to relieve the pressure on the brain. My most memorable Howe story was after the final game that season when we won the Stanley Cup and Gordie, his head shaved, came out on the ice after getting out of the hospital. It was quite a moving thing and the fans at Olympia went wild."

From near death on an operating table, Howe bounced back with the best season of his young career.

Some of the greatest players in history wore

the red-and-white of Detroit when the Red Wings were the scourge of the NHL, winning four Stanley Cups in six years beginning in 1950. Nine future members of the Hall of Fame played on those teams, and the coach, Tommy Ivan, and general manager, Jack Adams, also are enshrined. But there was only one signature superstar: Gordie Howe.

Every season in the 1950's, Howe led the Red Wings in goals. Only once in 14 seasons, beginning in 1950-51, did he not lead the club in total points. But his impact went beyond goals, assists, points and other bare statistics. Howe was the mainspring, the heart, the soul, the conscience of the Red Wings.

There's probably never been a greater judge of hockey talent in the game's history than Adams, the architect who molded and guided the Red Wings during the glory years.

"Plain and simple, Gordie Howe is the greatest thing that has appeared in hockey in 25 years," said Adams, who seldom offered tribute.

Of all the similarities between Howe and Yzerman, the most glaring disparity between

them is one of omission. Howe's name is etched on hockey's most prized silver chalice four times. Yzerman's is missing. In a career that needs no apologies, it is the final quest. Other great players have endured not winning the Stanley Cup. It is not a blot on their careers, for great careers cannot be so easily dismissed. But hockey players, especially great hockey players, are never quite whole without a championship ring.

The Red Wings and their captain are getting closer. The near-misses in 1994 and 1995 attest to it. They are willing to make no small sacrifices to reach, finally, hockey's Holy Grail. Steve Yzerman knows what it means.

"I sit and watch every year as the Stanley Cup is being presented to someone else," he said a couple of years ago. "That's really the one thing I'd be disappointed about in my career if I didn't win it. It'd be like playing tennis your whole life and never winning Wimbledon. I talk to guys who have won it. I realize what it means."

Like a sheet of ice on a remote encampment somewhere in Canada — Flin Flon, Moose Jaw, Smithers, Red Deer, and all those little prairie towns with wonderful names — is a birthright to young Canadian boys, so is the Stanley Cup.

Gordie Howe, the greatest Red Wing of all, achieved the glory.

Now the challenge is left to Steve Yzerman, and it makes him realize how much he really wants it, how much it would mean to be the signature player on the Red Wings team that nearly a half century later fulfilled its ancestral obligation and finally bridged the gap between the glory years of the 1950's — the Gordie Howe years — and the present.

Power and Silk.

Chapter Four

A Courageous Fan

By Cynthia Lambert

Some players crave the spotlight. Others quietly go about their business, seeking the satisfaction that comes with a job well done.

Then there are those who attempt to deflect attention, not needing or wanting recognition for their compassion and concern. But sometimes that is impossible, particularly when a good deed or special event becomes known. That was the case of the special bond between Steve Yzerman and a young girl afflicted with Ewings Sarcoma, a form of bone cancer.

Yzerman's relationship with Elysia Pefley began because, in part, of his need to give something back.

To embark on such an endeavor, a person has to first realize how much of an impact their presence can make. A smiling face is nearly always welcomed by a sick child, but it is a prominent face that can create magic. Yzerman has that distinction, that quality, and it has created magical moments for years.

"I've gone to hospitals ever since I came here to the Red Wings (in 1983)," Yzerman said. "On occasion (the team) would ask us to go. When I was younger, about 18 or so, I was more uncomfortable, but it's easier now."

Yzerman first met Elysia on Jan. 30, 1992 at St. John's Hospital in Detroit. It was the day Elysia began chemotherapy, an attempt to prolong her life, but not save it.

And it was a day a ray of unexpected sunlight flooded into Elysia's room.

"I was there to see another kid," Yzerman said. "I was kind of on my way out and they asked me to come in and say hi to another kid. That's how we first met. It was so long ago, I don't really remember any other details."

But Elysia's parents, Ralph and Anita, remember. Elysia, a hockey fan, looked up to see the captain of the Red Wings approaching her. Yzerman chatted with her, helping to distract from the events of the day. No serum, children's game or clown could have done a better job or had such a lasting effects.

"Elysia just beamed," Anita Pefley said. "After Steve left that first day, she just looked at me and said, 'I like him, mom.' From that point on, Yzerman was her guy.

"I remember the Wings had a game that Feb. 13. The kids from her school bought her a Steve

Elysia Pefley and her
hero, Steve Yzerman.

Elysia receives a Red Wings jersey and hockey stick from Yzerman in 1995.

Yzerman jersey and tickets to the game that night. After the game she insisted he sign her jersey. We had to stand there outside — and it was 30-below — waiting for Steve to come out. When he did come out, he saw her. All he had to do was smile at her and she was hooked."

Yzerman brought Elysia to practices, visited her at her home, rode with her on the Zamboni (a move which building manager Al Sobotka was reprimanded for), and even asked her to join him and his daughter, Isabella, for a skate.

And Yzerman talked with her, rarely getting replies, but knowing his presence was appreciated. The talks seldom dealt with her illness.

"I would ask her how she was feeling," Yzerman said. "She was always so quiet and shy. When I'd visit she would never really say much."

Over time, more Red Wings warmed to Elysia, the tiny girl with the dazzling eyes, smooth head and wide smile. Through her new friendships with members of the team, she was able to see most of the Red Wings' home games.

Elysia also developed a special relationship with former Red Wing Keith Primeau, who, like Yzerman, used his celebrity status to help others. There were nights when Primeau could be seen carrying the weary child out to her family's car, too weak to walk on her own, in too much pain to notice what was happening around her.

"Keith was real special to Elysia, too," Anita said. "But she treated Keith different. She talked to Keith; she stared at Steve."

When Red Wings players had a hard time finding tickets for Elysia, others would come through. Corporations donated their tickets, one physician gave the Pefley's his seats for an exhibition game against Montreal at the start of the 1995-96 season.

Sitting behind the goal, Elysia made a new friend in former Canadiens goalie Patrick Roy. And at the end of the game, Roy banged his stick on the glass to get Elysia's attention. Then he handed his stick over the glass to her, unable to resist her charm.

One night in the spring of 1994, after undergoing a bone marrow transplant — a procedure that is not only painful but debilitating — Elysia asserted herself again, showing the determination that allowed her to defy all odds against a disease that had claimed her body.

"She had just had a bone marrow transplant at (the University of Michigan) and she needed to be on an I.V. to get antibiotics because of an infection that resulted," Anita said. "But the Red Wings had a playoff game that night and she wanted to be there. She had to see Steve. But before she could go, she had to have a catheter in her chest removed. She had it removed with no anesthesia, because if they used any she would have missed the start of the game. It was so painful, but it was worth it to her.

"She had to see that game and everyone in the hospital knew what it meant to her. What you have to understand is that Steve gave her a reason to live. No matter how sick she was, she wanted to be where he was."

And Yzerman wanted her around. He took many steps to include Elysia in his life, with his wife, Lisa, and Isabella.

One of the most touching moments for Elysia occurred in January 1996, when she joined Yzerman at the National Athletic Awards at the Fox Theater in Detroit. Yzerman, who had advance notice that he narrowly defeated fellow Detroit athletes Herman Moore of the Lions, Grant Hill of the Pistons and Travis Fryman of the Tigers, was accompanied by Elysia on stage to receive his award.

"It was kind of set up, that she would be there to kind of present the award to me," Yzerman said, smiling. "I think she was nervous being in front of all of those people."

When Yzerman accepted his award, he had his left arm around Elysia's shoulder and introduced her to the audience.

"This is somebody pretty special to me, a good friend of mine," Yzerman said, as Elysia stared up at her idol, her affection clear to everyone.

"You talk about strength and courage," Yzerman said. "Elysia is probably the strongest person, most courageous person I know. And I am proud to be her friend."

Yzerman told the audience that in the next month, Elysia would celebrate her 11th birthday. He then handed her a small, brightly wrapped package — his present to her.

"It was a locket," Anita said. "A beautiful, gold, heart-shaped locket. She would never let me see what was inside. She said it was her and Steve's secret. Steve had something inscribed in it, and then he insisted it stay with her."

When Elysia was first diagnosed with Ewings Sarcoma, her family was told that she had a 10 percent chance of living longer than a year. Elysia, through her unwillingness to give in and because of her undying affection for Steve Yzerman, lived more than four years.

"If it weren't for Steve I think she would have fought hard, but not as much," Anita said. "She always fought to get to the next game, the next time she could see Steve. He gave her that extra kick."

Elysia died on March 17, 1996, while watching a televised broadcast of a Red Wings home game against Calgary. At about the time of her death, the scoreboard lights at Joe Louis Arena flickered, without explanation.

Later that week, Elysia was buried, wearing the heart-shaped locket that confirmed and sealed the relationship she shared with her buddy, Steve Yzerman.

Chapter Five

The Hero of Hockeytown

By Terry Foster
....

He is a quiet man.

Although when moved to be, he can be a man of many words, and the stories he spins are usually deliberate, in muffled and hushed tones.

But here is what I remember most about Red Wings great Steve Yzerman. The wild and delirious sounds of silent Steve:

Crack!

Clank!

Roar!

Let's go to the second round of the 1996 Stanley Cup playoffs against the St. Louis Blues, when doubt rang in every Red Wings fan.

It is Game 7 of a scoreless contest at Joe Louis Arena, which seemed to turn on every pass of the puck and every spectacular save by Chris Osgood and Jon Casey.

Talk about tension.

Yzerman crosses the blue line, winds up and lets loose a blistering shot that rises every inch of the way to the net.

Crack!

He had good wood on it. Maybe it was too good and would be another in a series of off-target shots.

You could hear the meeting of wood with rubber, even through the loud and worried moans of the crowd. The puck traveled like one of those surface-to-air missiles.

Then came the second sound. The sound that said everything was OK.

Clank!

The puck sailed over Casey's right shoulder, smacked the piping and caromed into the net with such a force that Casey's water bottle soared into the air following the game- and series-winning goal.

And finally, the last sound.

Roar!!!!!!!!!!!!

The roar from the crowd vibrated throughout the city. The sound was one of hysteria and relief, but there was a sound that said this one came from

Yzerman at practice before the 1989 playoffs.

From left, Yzerman, Joe Dumars, Cecil Fielder and Barry Sanders at Tiger Stadium in 1990.

the captain.

This goal belonged to Steve Yzerman, which meant everyone shared in it. For Yzerman is more than a hockey player.

He is Detroit hockey. From the inner city of Detroit, where hockey is not followed closely, to the suburb of St. Clair Shores, where hockey is king, Yzerman is the Detroit Red Wings.

During the 1980's and 1990's, four athletes signified Detroit sports. They will forever be linked to their teams and the community. They all displayed style, class and the desire to win. These athletes also represented our city. It was as if they had a City of Detroit seal stamped on their hearts.

To me, the Pistons are Isiah Thomas. He was the heart and soul of the back-to-back championship teams.

Barry Sanders is the Detroit Lions. One of the best running backs in the game and a man, as quiet as he is, who cares about people.

Alan Trammell is the same with the Tigers. A man of class and humbleness.

And the Red Wings?

Easy choice.

Steve Yzerman.

Yzerman is more than a great hockey player. He is a great hockey player who represents our community.

Yzerman could easily take the money and run. He doesn't need to get involved. He doesn't need to visit hospitals or lend his name to worthy causes.

Yzerman, like other high-profile people, could just write a check and still be considered a great guy. But that is not enough for him.

He understands that his presence at a function is needed to help others.

Most of his charitable deeds go unreported. Yzerman prefers it that way. He is a private person, so that explains part of it. But mostly, Yzerman doesn't think it is a big deal.

It is what he is supposed to do.

The adoption of Yzerman came early. In my mind, he is no longer a Canadian citizen, although he has played for Team Canada. He is no longer a resident of Ottawa, although he was nearly traded there because the Senators felt he could help them win and sell tickets.

Yzerman is a Detroiter, and with that comes full privileges.

What that means is people from Detroit are proud of their community and a little protective. When national publications slam our city we take it personally. When someone shuns one of our heroes, it is as if they made a personal attack on the entire city.

That is the way I felt when Mike Keenan cut Yzerman from Team Canada in 1987. He not only removed Yzerman from the team, but he kicked our city.

The NHL did the same thing last season when it did not include his name on the All-Star ballot. A Detroit radio host began a write-in campaign for Yzerman and collected nearly 100,000 ballots.

Detroit fans were angry and wanted to send a message to the league. The next season, Yzerman was on the ballot.

Yzerman is like a distant brother. If someone disrespects family, then they have to deal with all of the brothers, sisters, cousins, aunts and uncles, and nephews.

Keenan is still booed at Joe Louis Arena, in part for his decision to cut Yzerman from that Canada Cup team.

Red Wings coach Scotty Bowman felt the fans' wrath a year ago when he talked with the Ottawa Senators about a trade involving Yzerman.

The backlash was more than Bowman bargained for. The talk shows screamed for Bowman's hide and begged that Yzerman not be traded.

Yzerman was one of us and was not to be ridiculed and shipped out like a piece of lumber. He deserves better.

The people spoke not because Yzerman was a great player. The people spoke because Yzerman was a great human being and was one of us.

Bowman backed off on the trade in one of his best public-relations moves since he became coach. On the night of the 1995-96 season opener, the Joe Louis Arena crowd let Bowman know how they felt.

It gave Yzerman the longest and loudest ovation since the building opened. This was Detroit pouring its heart out to a brother, letting Yzerman know the people had his slack and would support him through thick and thin.

When Bowman's name was mentioned, boos rang through the air.

The message was simple.

"Mess with Steve Yzerman and you must deal with us."

Even when the national media omitted Yzerman's name when talking about great players, we took offense. Yes, Mario Lemieux and Wayne Gretzky are great. But what about Steve Yzerman?

It was as if they were slighting Detroit again.

In the beginning, I was not in favor of Yzerman being team captain. He was too young and did not understand the importance and responsibility of leadership. There were older players better prepared for that role.

Yzerman did not seem comfortable at first. He

Yzerman, in the spotlight, during the pregame playoff introductions in 1989.

appeared to be the reluctant leader. But the Red Wings were making a statement.

"You are the franchise player."

It is the role Grant Hill is growing into with the Pistons.

Initially, Yzerman's job was to score goals and win games. Then you could see his game slowly evolve. The 50- and 60-goal seasons were fine, but they become empty.

It earned him All-Star berths, notoriety and fat contracts. But you could see something begin to burn in Yzerman's eyes. After so many years of playoff frustration, he wanted to be a champion.

He became more vocal and tried to light a fire under teammates during the 1995 Stanley Cup Finals, which ended in a four-game sweep by New Jersey.

The ending was disappointing to Red Wings fans, but I saw the hunger in Yzerman's belly. It was good to see. He had finally turned from a play-

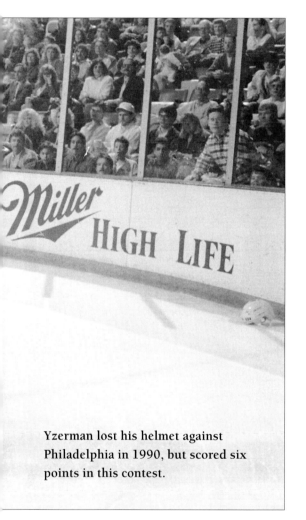

Yzerman lost his helmet against Philadelphia in 1990, but scored six points in this contest.

nament was that Yzerman lacked the speed to keep up with teammates. They talked about shipping him home.

The next thing you hear, Yzerman is scoring a winning goal in overtime. Yzerman deserves a championship dance with the Stanley Cup because he made the sacrifices necessary to achieve greatness.

It has gotten to the point where it seems as if some unknown hockey god is playing a cruel trick on Yzerman and the rest of the Red Wings. No matter how great they play during the regular season, some demon trips them up in the playoffs, denying Yzerman his final, crowning moment.

I am not sure what plans the Red Wings have for Yzerman when he retires. It was disappointing to see Thomas retire and not become the promised Piston-for-life, as we were told.

It is important that a role be found for Yzerman with the Red Wings. It is important that he remains here and remains a part of this community.

His play inspired many youngsters to take up the game. His charity work has made this city a better place to live for some who don't have it so well.

Yzerman has even helped bring hockey to the African-American community, which wants to know a little more about the man with the quick wrist shot and superior skating ability.

Yzerman is family now. Detroit is stamped on his heart, and even when his career ends, we don't want to let go of what he built here.

to the point where some believe he has lost a couple of steps. That might be true, but if you look at his total game, Yzerman has played his best two-way hockey the last two seasons. He has made adjustments to age and, of course, Bowman.

He has even spoken up in the locker room, encouraging teammates to elevate their games.

Yzerman is a fighter, and a little tougher than we give him credit for. The word out of the Team Canada camp during the 1996 World Cup tour-

Ten to

First Goal, *Oct. 5, 1983*

First Hat Trick, *Dec. 23, 1983*

Season Ends Early, *March 1, 1988*

28-Game Point Streak, *Jan. 4, 1989*

Six-point Game, *March 15, 1989*

Natural Hat Trick, *Nov. 17, 1990*

1,000th Point, *Feb. 24, 1993*

remember

500th Goal, *Jan. 17, 1996*

Five-point Playoff Game, *May 5, 1996*

Playoff Overtime Hero, *May 16, 1996*

From the Sports Pages of

The Detroit News

Oct. 5, 1983: Wings 6, Jets 6

Yzerman Scores First NHL Goal

No. 1 Pick Stars in Debut

By Vartan Kupelian
....

The Detroit News

Winnipeg, Manitoba, Oct. 5, 1983 — The Detroit Red Wings accomplished their goal last night. Ed Mio wants to know what overtime accomplished.

The Red Wings opened the 1983-84 season with a 6-6 tie against the Winnipeg Jets when the newly instituted five-minute overtime failed to produce a winner.

"It was a good point, we'll take it," said Danny Gare, the Red Wings captain, who was one of six Detroit players to score. "There were a lot of good signs — the young kids played well, the goalie made saves when we needed 'em and we got goals from all four lines. Winnipeg is a good skating club and we skated with them. And we came back and got goals when we needed 'em."

The Red Wings, never thrilled with the concept of overtime to begin with, were forced into the extra time when Doug Smail scored at 16:37 of the final period.

After a two-minute rest, the teams switched ends and played five more minutes.

The Jets missed a chance from the opening face-off and later Mio, the new Detroit goalie, stopped Bengt Lundholm on a breakaway at 1:32 of the overtime.

The Wings' best chance belonged to the Steve Yzerman line two minutes into the session. Yzerman, the 18-year-old center who was Detroit's No. 1 pick in this year's entry draft, scored his first NHL goal and set up Eddie Johnstone's goal at 9:11 of the final period to give the Wings a 6-5 lead.

"Tell me, what did the overtime prove?" Mio asked.

"Everybody just tried not to make a mistake. If you don't score in the first two minutes, then you just wait for it to end. If you do make a mistake, it's 60 minutes of hard work gone. And that's what that stuff at the end was all about. The guy missed a goal and all that was was frustration. Then the game ends, he goes crazy."

The Jets have been billed in the preseason as a big, aggressive team and they tried to muscle the Red Wings. The game ended with Paul MacLean, the player foiled by Mio, and Detroit's Greg Smith fighting and both benches emptying. Peace was quickly restored, but not before Mio made his point.

The Red Wings' other goal scorers against

Winnipeg goalie Doug Soetaert were Ivan Boldirev, Dwight Foster and John Ogrodnick. Reed Larson had three assists.

Yzerman, who struggled through the exhibition games, was a standout. And, at times, he was even spectacular.

"We should have won. We outplayed them," said Yzerman, who was taking the blame for Smail's second goal. "I sort of let down on my check and the guy went in and scored.

"I felt more comfortable but I still have things to work on. The week to practice and get ready helped and it was an advantage to play on the road."

Scott Arniel scored three goals for the Jets. MacLean had the other. Johnstone said he didn't even see the puck skip past Soetaert on his goal, which almost stood up.

"I just got to the net as best I could," said the veteran right winger, who came from the New York Rangers with Mio and Rog Duguay in the big off-season deal.

"Then I ended up in the corner on my back. Stevie made a heckuva play. He came out around the defenseman and put the puck in front. I whacked it as hard as I could."

"The effort was definitely there. If we play with that intensity and clean up some of the mental errors ..."

"A lot of good things got done out there," added Boldirev. "We came back when we were down."

Arniel's third goal, at 1:16 of the third period, gave Winnipeg a 5-4 lead, but Ogrodnick wiped that out at 2:29, with Boldirev and Duguay assisting.

A youthful Yzerman discusses a penalty with a referee.

Yzerman powers a slap shot — his
signature — past a defender.

Wings 6, Jets 6

Detroit	3	1	2	0	6
Winnipeg	1	3	2	0	6

First period

1, Winnipeg, Arniel 1 (Boschman, Babych), :33. 2, Detroit, Boldirev 1 (Melrose, Gare) 4:36. 3, Detroit, Gare 1 (Larson), 8:43. 4, Detroit, Yzerman 1 (Johnstone, Manno), 11:41. Penalties — Manno, Det, 14:66; Larson, Det, major, minor, 15:44; MacLean, Win, major, minor, 15:55.

Second period

5, Winnipeg, Smail 1 (Lundholm, Maxwell), 1:01. 6, Winnipeg, Arniel 2 (Boschman, Steen), 7:27. 7, Detroit, Foster 1 (Nolan, Larson), 12:32. 8, Winnipeg, MacLean 1 (Mullen, Babych), 19:22. Penalties — Park, Det, 5:33, Babych, Win, 10:19.

Third period

9, Winnipeg, Arniel 3 (Boschman, Deblois), 1:16. 10, Detroit, Ogrodnick 1 (Boldirev, Duguay), 2:29. 11, Detroit, Johnstone 1 (Yzerman, Larson), 9:11. 12, Winnipeg, Smail 2 (Watters, Steen), 16:37. Penalties — Melrose, Det, major, minor, 3:01; Campbell, Det, 3:01; Maxwell, Win, major, minor, game misconduct, 3:01; Steen, Win, 4:44; Manno, Det, major, 15:20; Deblois, Win, major, 15:20.

Overtime

No Scoring. Penalties — Smith, Det, 5:00; MacLean, Win, 5:00.

Shots on goal

Detroit	7	11	7	2	27
Winnipeg	5	15	11	3	34

Dec. 23, 1983: Wings 9, Maple Leafs 2

Yzerman Gets First Hat Trick

Winless Streak Snapped at 11 as Leafs Fall, 9-2

By Vartan Kupelian

....

The Detroit News

Detroit, Dec. 23, 1983 — The Detroit Red Wings put a little merry back into their Christmas last night.

Make that a little merry and a lot of goals.

With John Ogrodnick and Steve Yzerman each scoring three goals, the Red Wings treated themselves to a 9-2 victory over the Toronto Maple Leafs at Joe Louis Arena.

For the first time in 27 days and a dozen games, the Wings did enough things well enough often enough to end an 11-game winless streak.

Ogrodnick, who shares the club goal-scoring lead with Yzerman — each has 22 — added two assists for a five-point night.

Yzerman, the spectacular 18-year-old rookie, notched an assist in addition to his first career

hat trick to finish with four points, and Ron Duguay had three points, including a short-handed goal.

Ed Johnstone and Reed Larson joined the goal-scoring parade, with Ivan Boldirev, Brad Park and Greg Smith each drawing two assists as the Wings pulled out of a month-long tailspin. Park was honored in pregame ceremonies marking his 1,000th regular-season game.

Goaltender Greg Stefan snapped a personal six-game losing streak, turning aside 26 Toronto shots and drawing the lone assist on Larson's goal at 18:48 of the third period, the last of Detroit's five third-period goals.

Stefan said the winless streak had left the Red Wings "pretty tense."

"But actually there was a good feeling going

With a defender on his heels, Yzerman chases after a puck.

into this game," he said. "We had a meeting yesterday and pulled things together. Everybody was so psyched."

Defensively, the Wings blanked an old nemesis, Rick Vaive — who had scored 13 goals in his last 10 games against Detroit — and shut off the Maple Leaf power play, the NHL's top-rated unit, when it counted. The Leafs finally got a power-play goal by Bill Derlago, but not until they were four goals down.

On top of that, Duguay scored his shorthanded goal at 7:24, with the Red Wings playing with only three skaters in front of Stefan, to Toronto's four.

Gary Nylund scored the other Leafs goal in the third period.

"It's a good feeling to get," Coach Nick Polano said after the rout. "I hope we can get a couple of more (wins).

"What did I say to them? About 105 things ... it would take too long to repeat them.

"If you can stop Toronto's power play—they've got by far the best in the league—you have a chance to beat 'em," said Polano, whose team has a rematch with the Leafs on Monday night in Toronto.

Park became only the third active player to reach the 1,000-game plateau, joining Philadelphia's Bobby Clarke and the New York Islanders' Butch Goring. Goring beat Park to it by three days.

Going into the 1996-97 season Yzerman had scored 18 hat tricks.

Alex Delvecchio, former Red Wing star and Hall of Famer who is second (1,549 games) behind only Gordie Howe (1,767) in games played, presented Park with the milestone award.

The Red Wings treated the brave, but chilled, crowd of 15,377 to three power-play goals in the first period.

Ogrodnick and Yzerman scored a minute apart, and Ogrodnick added his second goal with eight seconds left in the period.

Toronto's Stewart Gavin went off for holding at 11:45, and Ogrodnick opened the scoring 22 seconds later, converting Duguay's pass.

At 12:55, Vaive was penalized for tripping. This time, the Red Wings needed just nine seconds to score.

Ogrodnick sent the puck back to the left point to Yzerman, who teed it up and whistled

a shot past Toronto goalie Mike Palmateer.

Referee Bruce Hood's third straight penalty against the Leafs went to Terry Martin for tripping at 18:00.

Yzerman and rookie linemate Lane Lambert combined to make it 4-0 early in the second period. Yzerman scored on a pass from Lambert at 2:36.

The Maple Leafs finally got on the scoreboard at 7:17 with Derlago beating Stefan on a power play.

Wings 9, Leafs 2

Toronto	0	1	1	2
Detroit	3	1	5	9

First period

1, Detroit, Ogrodnick 20 (Duguay, Boldirev) 12:07 (pp). 2, Detroit, Yzerman 20 (Ogrodnick, Duguay), 13:17 (pp). 3, Detroit, Ogrodnick 21 (Yzerman, Park) 19:52 (pp). Penalties — Nolan, Det, 8:45; Gavin, Tot, 11:45; Vaive, Tor, 12:55; Martin, Tor, 13:00.

Second period

4, Detroit, Yzerman 21 (Lambert, Park) 2:36. 5, Toronto, Derlago 15 (Ihnacek, Gingras), 7:17 (pp). Penalties — Nolan, Det, 3:28; Campbell, Det, 5:19; Nylund, Tor, misconduct, 9:46; Stewart, Tor, 11:47; Duguay, Det, minor-misconduct, 11:47; Gingras, Tor, 13:50.

Third period

6, Detroit, Duguay 11, 7:24 (sh). 7, Detroit, Yzerman 22 (Ogrodnick, Boldirev), 10:48 (pp). 8, Detroit, Ogrodnick 22 (Craven, G. Smith), 13:20. 9, Detroit, Johnstone 7 (Dunlap, G. Smith), 13:31. 10, Toronto, Nylund 1 (Daoust, Anderson), 18.08. 11, Detroit, Larson 10 (Stefan), 18:48. Penalties — Benning, Tor, 2:34, Ladouceur, Det, 4:58; Dunlap, Det, 6:23; Derlago, Tor, 6:48; Barrett, Det, 6:48; Nigro, Tor, 6:48; Palmateer, Tor, served by Martin, 18:20; Ladouceur, Det, 19:28.

Shots on goal

Toronto	7	13	8	28
Detroit	10	10	15	35

March 1, 1988: Wings 4, Sabres 0

Yzerman's Season Over

He Scores 50th Goal Before Injuring Knee

By Cynthia Lambert
....

The Detroit News

Detroit, March 1, 1988 — The worst thing that could possibly happen to the Red Wings happened Tuesday night. Although they defeated the Buffalo Sabres, 4-0, the Red Wings lost the services of All-Star center and captain Steve Yzerman for the rest of the regular season and the playoffs with a knee injury.

With 1:59 left in the second period, Yzerman cut in on Sabres goaltender Tom Barrasso. Buffalo defenseman Calle Johansson stopped Yzerman's progress with a clean check, sending Yzerman sliding across the ice toward the goal. Yzerman stopped by crashing his right knee into the goal post, knocking the net off its magnets. Yzerman attempted to get up, but instead fell to the ice, writhing in pain.

After being assisted off the ice by Red Wings physical therapist Jim Pengelly and teammate Doug Halward, Yzerman was taken to Detroit's Hutzel Hospital for an examination by Red Wings physician Dr. Robert Teitge. A preliminary diagnosis showed Yzerman has a severe strain of the posterior cruciate ligament, which connects the knee to the top of the calf.

Surgery was tentatively scheduled for today but could be postponed so the Red Wings can receive a second opinion.

But one thing won't change. Yzerman is out for the season.

"It's a tremendous tragedy to lose Stevie," said an emotional Red Wings coach Jacques Demers. "Stevie's our franchise. Not to take anything away from any of the other players, but Stevie has taken us to where we are now.

Wings 4, Sabres 0

First period

1, Detroit, Veitch 6 (Norwood, Yzerman), 14:09 (pp). Penalties—Krupp, Buf (interference), 13:23. Priestley, Buf (tripping) 16:21; Gallant, Det (slashing), 16:21; Hartman, Buf major (fighting), 18:48; Nill, Det major (fighting), 18:48.

Second period

2, Detroit, Yzerman 50, (Norwood, Klima), 3:26 (pp). Penalties—Halkidis, Buf (tripping), 2:18; Nill, Det (high-sticking), 5:57; Delorme, Det (roughing), 12:58, Burr, Det (roughing), 18:44.

Third period

3. Detroit, Halward 5 (Burr), 2:42. 4, Detroit, Gallant 28 (Oates, Barr), 17:33 (pp). Penalties—Delorme, Det (holding), 3:30; Andreychuk, Buf (roughing), 3:36, Nill, Det (roughing) 3:36, Halkidis, Buf (delay of game), 14:05: Probert, Det (interference), 14:36; Buffalo bench, served by Hogue (too many on ice), 15:49; Chiasson, Det (high-sticking), 18:17; Priestley, Buf (tripping), 19:29.

Shots on goal

Buffalo	6	7	6	19
Detroit	10	13	11	34

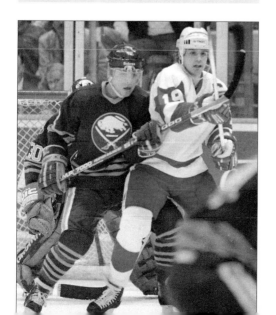

"I have to be honest with you. Before each game I pray that Stevie doesn't get hurt. The way he rushes to the net every night and cuts in toward the goal, you just have to hope that nothing like this ever happens."

But it did. And Demers, like several of the players, remember their reaction when they saw Yzerman bounce off the net and then painfully pound the ice with his left skate.

"I felt like I was shot," Demers said, staring ahead at the wall. "I felt like that and I'm sure the assistant coaches felt like that, and the players, too. I actually felt like someone shot me. I got all numb. I'm still numb. But I knew when he didn't get up, he was done. I knew it. I just knew it."

Getting lost in the shuffle was that Yzerman, at the beginning of the second period, gave the Red Wings a 2-0 lead with his 50th goal of the season — one of the few personal goals Yzerman would admit to wanting.

"At least he got his 50th," said Yzerman's close friend and teammate Gerard Gallant, who will replace Yzerman as team captain for the remainder of the season. "That would have been just awful if he hadn't scored his 50th. Just awful."

That goal, plus an assist, gave Yzerman a team-leading 102 points for the season. Gallant is second, with 28 goals and 34 assists for 62 points.

Also scoring for the Red Wings, who snapped a four-game losing streak with the victory, were Darren Veitch, Halward and Gallant.

Yzerman fights for position against a Buffalo defender.

After knee surgery, Yzerman hobbles to a plane to fly back to Detroit.

Without Yzerman, Wings' Mettle Will Be Tested

By Joe Falls

The Detroit News

It is the same as the Pistons losing Isiah Thomas.

The loss of Steve Yzerman is a crushing blow to the Red Wings, probably wrecking their season.

They should hang onto first place in the Norris Division but it's hard to see how they can make much of a mark in the playoffs.

You don't lose a player who has had a hand in almost 40 percent of your goals and not be crippled by it.

What happens, for instance, to Bob Probert, who has flourished as Yzerman's linemate? He'll probably play with Adam Oates and, suddenly, the game could become a terrible struggle for him.

With players the quality of Yzerman, you lose more than a body. In this case, the Red Wings lose the heart of their team, their on-the-ice leader, and now they must shake up the rest of the team to try to make up for his loss.

The truth is, they can't replace him and their season is probably lost.

The Red Wings have truly been a cursed hockey team, for it was only two years ago — when Yzer-man was showing his first real flashes of brilliance — that they lost him with a broken collarbone.

This time it is a knee injury — sustained in Tuesday night's 4-0 victory over Buffalo at Joe Louis Arena — that ended the season for him. Knees can be much more damaging than collarbones. Sometimes they don't mend properly and the athlete is left to labor for the rest of his career.

What this means is Jacques Demers will have to apply himself more than ever to hold his team together.

He had done a tremendous job of coaching the Red Wings this season, even better than a year ago. He has gotten incredible mileage out of some very ordinary talent. He is the reason the Red Wings are in first place.

Now he will have to push and prod more than ever, and if he wonders how to handle such things, he could put a call into Sparky Anderson in Lakeland, Fla., today for a bit of advice.

Anderson has the right idea about losing players, through injury or otherwise. Once they are gone, they are gone. He knows that no amount of crying can bring them back. You simply go on.

Demers' main job will be to convince his players they can make it without Yzerman. He always talks about their character. Now they can show it and do something for the man who has done so much for them.

Oates will probably be moved into Yzerman's center spot, between Petr Klima and Probert. That'll leave Shawn Burr to center Gerard Gallant and Dave Barr, with John Chabot centering the third line of Brent Ashton and Jim Nill.

Yzerman's injury is a terrible setback for him because he was having his first big season in five years. He never got going when Nick Polano was the coach. Remember how Polano pulled him on all the important faceoffs? Yzerman never had much confidence in those days. He was also very young.

For some reason, Yzerman never hit it off with Harry Neale in Neale's brief time as a coach. Their personalities didn't mesh — Yzerman being soft-spoken and withdrawn and Neal being outgoing and gregarious.

Yzerman started showing some life under Brad Park in his third season and was playing his best hockey when he ran into Lee Norwood when Norwood played for the St. Louis Blues and broke his collarbone.

It's been Demers who has brought out the best in Yzerman. Making him the captain was one thing, but permitting him to be himself — which is quiet and withdrawn — Demers allowed Yzerman to settle down and play his kind of hockey.

From being turned away twice by Team Canada in the series against the Soviets, Yzerman — with these 50 goals and 52 assists — has become one of the top players in the league.

When you think about it, the Pistons could replace Isiah Thomas easier than the Red Wings could replace Steve Yzerman.

That's how valuable he has become.

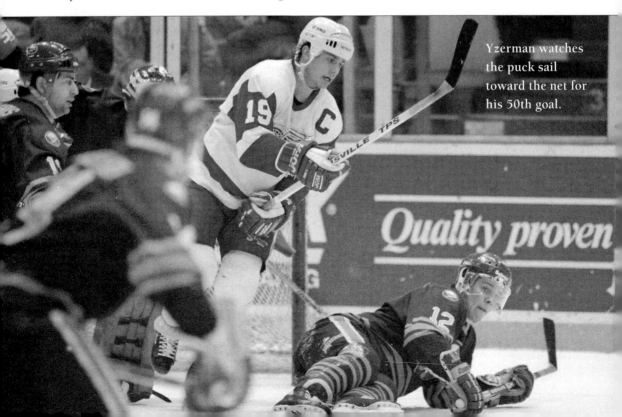

Yzerman watches the puck sail toward the net for his 50th goal.

Team Must Regroup After Losing Yzerman

By Cynthia Lambert

The Detroit News

Red Wings forward Tim Higgins sat in front of his locker after Tuesday night's game and stared at the center of the dressing room. The Red Wings had just taken a 4-0 decision over the Buffalo Sabres, but they had lost their leading scorer, Steve Yzerman, for the remainder of the season with a knee injury.

"The loss of Stevie is tremendous," Higgins said. "But we can't, as a team, think that right now. If we think that it's going to hurt us then it will. That's something we just can't let happen.

"Stevie's been a great player for us all season long. He was a great player and he never showed any fear. Right now everybody has to take a piece of Stevie inside them and play that much better. We have to take Stevie with us on that ice every night."

When told that his response sounded more like a eulogy than a strategy, Higgins chuckled.

"Well, Stevie is dead to us now as far as helping our hockey team," Higgins said. "It's almost like he's dead."

Even Red Wings general manager Jimmy Devellano tended to speak of Yzerman in the past tense in his postgame press conference.

"Every player has to pick up 5 percent to make up for the loss of Stevie," Devellano said. "He was the reason we are where we are."

Although it was difficult for Red Wings coach Jacques Demers to talk about anything but the loss of Yzerman, he did speculate on how the injury could have a positive effect on some of the Red Wings players.

"This will give Mel Bridgman the opportunity to play some center," Demers said. "It gives all our centers — Shawn Burr, Adam Oates, John Chabot — a chance to come up with some big games for us. We need them now like never before."

Jan. 4, 1989: Wings 4, Blues 2

Yzerman Extends Streak

Wings Chase Blues Away

By Cynthia Lambert

....

The Detroit News

Detroit, Jan. 4, 1989 — Trade threats served as inspiration for many Red Wings players Wednesday night.

The Red Wings returned to their grinding, patient game before a crowd of 19,711 at Joe Louis Arena and defeated the St. Louis Blues, 4-2, behind Gerard Gallant's fourth career hat trick.

The victory, which ended the Red Wings' four-game losing streak, was only the second in nine games for Detroit, which leads the Norris division with a 19-15-5 record.

But the player most rumored to be traded — Bob Probert — didn't respond at all. Instead, he

Yzerman, behind the net, waits to make a move against the St. Louis goal.

Wings 4, Blues 2

St. Louis	1	1	0	2
Detroit	1	2	1	4

First period

1, St. Louis, Zezel 10 (Gingras, Ronning), 1:04 (pp). 2 Detroit, Gallant 20 (Chiasson, Yzerman), 7:15 (pp). Penalties—Evans, StL (roughing), :42; Chiasson, Det (holding), :42; MacLean, Det (roughing), :42; Ewen, StL double minor-major (elbowing, roughing, fighting), 6:15; Houde, Det (roughing), 6:15; Norwood, Det, major game misconduct (fighting), 6:15; Gallant, Det (hooking), 12:06; Reglan, StL, double minor (roughing), 18:41; Pavese, Det (charging), 18:41.

Second period

3, St. Louis, Ronning 11, 3:17. 4 Detroit, Gallant 21 (Chiasson, Oates), 7:38. 5, Detroit, Gallant 22 (Barr), 14:24. Penalties—Ronning, StL (tripping), 1:06; Nill, Det (delay of game), 11:26.

Third period

6, Detroit, MacLean 24 (Gallant, Yzerman), 10:55. Penalties—P.Cavallini, StL (cross-checking), :41; Klima, Det (slashing), :41; Roberts, StL (holding), 5:27; Barr, Det (holding), 7:10; Hull, StL, (hooking), 8:17; Pavese, Det (elbowing), 11:16.

Shots on goal

St. Louis	11	12	11	34
Detroit	9	10	4	23

was benched for much of the third period because of his diminishing effect on the ice.

Probert was unavailable for comment, but his agent — Pat Ducharme — spoke at length with his client after the game.

"He didn't think he played all that well," said Ducharme. "I think he only got one shift in the third period."

But Gallant, one of the team's assistant captains, responded very well.

He switched lines, and the move seemed to improve his play. Gallant completed his hat trick at 14:24 in the second period, scoring once in the first and twice in the second.He also assisted on Paul MacLean's game-clinching goal midway through the third period.

Peter Zezel and Cliff Ronning scored for the struggling Blues (14-19-7), who lost their third consecutive game and eighth in their last 13 (2-8-3).

Red Wings coach Jacques Demers said he knew why Probert was so ineffective.

Yzerman and
his teammates
huddle after a
goal against
the Blues.

Yzerman, with two assists, extended his
point-scoring streak to 28 games, during which
time he has 29 goals and 36 assists for 65 points.
The 28 games tied Yzerman with four players
— Guy Lafleur, Wayne Gretzky, Mario Lemieux
and Paul Coffey — for the fourth-longest streak
in NHL history. The record, held by Gretzky, is
51 games.

March 15, 1989: Wings 8, Oilers 6

Slick Yzerman Upends Oilers

Impressive Empty-Net Goal is "Icing on the Cake"

By Cynthia Lambert

The Detroit News

Edmonton, Alberta, March 15, 1989 — Steve Yzerman did it again.

But it wasn't just his first-ever NHL six-point performance, which led the Red Wings to a 8-6 victory over the Stanley Cup champion Edmonton Oilers, that dumbfounded his teammates and opponents Wednesday night.

It was his perfectly executed chip shot over Oilers defenseman Kevin Lowe, which resulted in his second goal of the game and gave Detroit its final goal with 21 seconds to play.

With Detroit leading, 7-6, and 53 seconds left to play, Oilers replacement goaltender Grant Fuhr left the net for the extra attacker. Gerard Gallant flipped the puck to Yzerman, who popped the puck over Lowe.

And as the puck tumbled into the empty net,

the Red Wings players on the bench chuckled.

"How did he do that?" asked Red Wings forward Tim Higgins. "The guy (Lowe) was going to block the shot, so Stevie just made a chip shot over him. The guy was right in front of him. I don't know how Stevie did that. Incredible."

"I was right behind him, I knew what he was going to try and do," said Oilers center Jimmy Carson, a Grosse Pointe Woods native, who also scored two goals Wednesday. "I knew what he was thinking. He didn't want to take the shot, because it would just hit Kevin. So he popped it up. That's something you try at practice; I know I do. But I've never done it in a game. Not like that."

In typical Yzerman fashion, the Red Wings captain played down the goal after the game. "I

Yzerman battles with
an Edmonton defender
near the net.

Yzerman waits for the Edmonton offense to cross the center line.

didn't want to blast it because he was right there," he said. "My main concern was to get it in deep. I just flipped it up in the air. It was a sigh of relief that it went in. If it doesn't, who knows? They could come back and score and tie it up."

As Yzerman, who now has 63 goals and 146 points, was swarmed by reporters in the visitors dressing room at the Northlands Coliseum, defenseman Lee Norwood and right wing Joe

Kocur sat across the room on a bench and watched the scene.

"Hey, I got an assist," Norwood said.

"I did, too," Kocur added.

With that, the two smiled at each other, shook hands and turned their attention back to the scene across the room.

"It was a very nice approach shot," Norwood said, mimicking a TV golf commentator.

Wings 8, Oilers 6

Detroit	2	3	3	8
Edmonton	0	4	2	6

First period

1, Detroit, Robertson 3 (Zombo, Burr), 8:27; 2, Detroit, Yzerman 62 (Gallant), 12:57. Penalties — Robertson, Det (boarding), 13:15; Gregg, Edm (holding), 14:47.

Second period

3, Edmonton, Simpson 34 (Messier, Anderson) 5:17. 4, Edmonton, Muni 5 (McClelland, Buchberger), 5:39. 5, Edmonton, Carson 46 (Huddy, Messier), 9:17. 6, Detroit, Chiasson 11 (Yzerman, Houda), 10:30; 7, Edmonton, Simpson 36 (Huddy, Messier), 15:37 (pp). 8, Detroit, Gallant 37 (Yzerman, Barr), 19:34 (pp). 9, Detroit, Burr 17 (Kocur), 19:49. Penalties — Chiasson, Det (tripping), 7:07; Kocur, Det major (fighting), 12:28, Buchberger, Edm. major (fighting), 12:28; Yzerman, Det (tripping), 14:52; Muni, Edm (high-sticking), 18:25.

Third period

10, Edmonton, Kurri 40 (Tikkanen, Carson), 3:16. 11, Detroit, Chabot 2 (Yzerman, Zombo), 7:07 (sh). 12, Edmonton, Carson 47 (Kurri, Lowe), 12:02. 13, Detroit, MacLean 34 (Yzerman, Gallant), 18:31. 14, Detroit, Yzerman 63 (Gallant, Norwood), 19:39. Penalties — Kocur, Det (interference), 6:24; Yzerman, Det (slashing), 13:24.

Shots on goal

Detroit	11	6	13	30
Edmonton	4	9	12	25

"That's an eagle for sure," Kocur added.

Regardless of the interpretation, it was the finishing touch on a wild game that touched on every facet of hockey.

In the first period, there was tight checking by both sides. Still, the Red Wings took a 2-0 lead into the second period on goals by Yzerman and Torri Robertson — his first as a Red Wing.

That's when the wide-open style began. By the end of the second period, the Red Wings held a 5-4 lead, thanks to goals by Steve Chiasson, Gallant (power play) and Shawn Burr.

Former Michigan State standout Craig Simpson scored twice for Edmonton in the period, and Craig Muni and Carson accounted for the others.

When the third period began, the Oilers changed goalies, removing Bill Ranford and replacing him with the experienced Fuhr.

Jari Kurri and Carson sandwiched goals around a short-handed goal by Detroit's John Chabot by 12:02 of the third to create a 6-6 tie.

But Paul MacLean tipped in an Yzerman pass at 18:31 to give the Red Wings the 7-6 lead and set up Yzerman's unique empty-net goal.

"That chip shot at the end of the game was the icing on the cake," Red Wings coach Jacques Demers said. "I don't know if he used a nine-iron or what. But that's Steve. He keeps on doing those things."

Demers Campaigns on Road for Yzerman

By Cynthia Lambert

....

The Detroit News

Red Wings coach Jacques Demers knows Steve Yzerman is the heart and soul of his team.

But now he wants his captain to be voted the Hart and soul, as in the Hart Trophy as the league's MVP.

The story line is familiar to Red Wings fans, but every new arena, every multiple-point Yzerman performance, Demers states his case to the visiting press. Actually, it's not a bad ploy, considering it's the hockey writers who vote on the MVP.

"Now you see why I keep talking about Steve Yzerman and why he should be the MVP," Demers told about a dozen reporters after Yzerman's six points led the Red Wings to an 8-6 victory over the Edmonton Oilers. He does it all for this team. He definitely should have very, very strong consideration."

Said Yzerman's linemate, Paul MacLean, "He's been the dominant player on this team all season. He's a great player."

Numbers game: The Wings victory over the Oilers was notable for more than just the two points. Because the Oilers scored six goals, a Wings' win was against the odds.

Going into the game, the Oilers were 30-7-2 when they scored four or more goals. They are 5-21-5 when they score less than four goals.

Trivia question: Last season, Bob Probert led the league in penalty minutes with 398. Who leads the Red Wings this season?

Home-grown star: Edmonton Oiler Jimmy Carson, who grew up in Grosse Pointe Woods, is going after a record of distinction in the Oilers' last seven games of the regular season. He now has 47 goals and must score three more to become only the second player in NHL history to have two 50-goal seasons before he turns 21. The first, of course, was Wayne Gretzky.

"I would like to get it," said Carson, who was traded to Edmonton from Los Angeles in the deal that sent Gretzky to the Kings. "I've got a very good shot at it. There's no question about that. It's a nice mark. I'll just have to keep working hard. I'd be very disappointed if I didn't get it, especially being so close."

Trivia answer: Gallant leads the Wings in time spent in the "Sin Bin" with 214 minutes. Gallant's NHL high came last season, with 242 minutes in 73 games.

Still, Gallant was the team's second-leading scorer (Steve Yzerman had 102 points) with 34 goals and 39 assists for 73 points.

Two of hockey's best:
Yzerman closely guards
Edmonton's Mark Messier.

Nov. 17, 1990: Wings 8, Leafs 4

Yzerman Records Natural Hat Trick

Four-Point Period Highlights Win Over Leafs

By Cynthia Lambert
....

The Detroit News

Toronto, Nov. 17, 1990 — The Maple Leafs were up to their old tricks, and so was Steve Yzerman in Detroit's 8-4 victory Saturday night.

Against a sluggish defense, Yzerman weaved his way to his most productive game of the season, netting a natural (uninterrupted) hat trick by 11:59 of the first period and drawing first assists on goals by Joe Kocur and Bobby Dollas. It was Detroit's first victory on the road (1-7-3) and ended its five-game losing streak.

Toronto had had a two-game winning streak.

"I guess I found out tonight that Steve can play fairly regularly," said a smiling Coach Bryan Murray, who used Yzerman to center two lines. "I was hoping he would come up with a game like this, and I know Steve was hoping so, too."

The goals — numbers 11, 12 and 13 — gave Yzerman his 10th career hat trick. Moreover, his assist on Kocur's goal near the end of the period allowed him to join three former Red Wings — Joe Carveth, Mickey Redmond and John Ogrodnick — in the record book for most points in a period. Three goals in a period has been accomplished by several players in Detroit history, including Yzerman in 1988 and 1985.

"He had a heck of a game, a heck of a start," Toronto defensemen Brad Marsh said of the Detroit captain. "Tonight we didn't do a very good job of checking him. Tonight he pretty much won the game for them in the first period.

"No one has done a good job (checking him) since he came into the league. I don't think you can put the onus on one guy. When you play against a guy like Wayne Gretzky or Mario

Wings 8, Leafs 4

Detroit	4	1	3	8
Toronto	0	1	3	4

First period

1, Detroit, Yzerman 11 (Barr, Green), 2:21. 2, Detroit, Yzerman 12 (Green), 10:53. 3, Detroit, Yzerman 13 (McKay), 11:59. 4, Detroit, Kocur 4 (Yzerman, McKay), 19:19. Penalties — Fedyk, Det (roughing), 11:35; Ramage, Tor (roughing), 11:35; Zombo, Det (interference), 14:02, Racine, Det (holding), 16:47.

Second period

5, Detroit, Dollas 1 (Yzerman, Barr), 4:25. 6, Toronto, Ellett 5 (Ramage, Hannan), 13:46 (pp). Penalties — Burr, Det (holding), 1:51; Marois, Tor (slashing) 1:51, McKay, Det (holding) 6:36; Yzerman, Det, misconduct, 6:36; Damphousse, Tor (slashing), 8:55; Chiasson, Det (holding), 12:08; McCrimmon, Det, major-game misconduct (high-sticking), 12:24; Burr, Det (roughing), 19:48; Clark, Tor double minor (high-sticking, roughing), 19:48.

Third period

7, Detroit, Burr 7 (Racine, Djoos), 1:51. 8, Toronto, Maguire 4 (Ramage), 3:38. 9, Toronto, Fenton 6 (Shedden, Clark), 10:13. 10, Detroit, Fedorov 9 (Carson, Burr), 12:08. 11, Toronto, Marois 8 (Damphousse, Krushelnyski), 14:34. 12, Detroit, Fedorov 10 (Burr, Cheveldae), 19:11. Penalties — none.

Shots on goal

Detroit	10	9	14	33
Toronto	13	15	9	37

Lemieux, you need five guys working to stop him. And tonight, we didn't do a very good job on him. Obviously."

But not much can stop Yzerman when he has the determination that he did Saturday. Part of it stemmed from his belief that he had not been contributing as much as he should. That comes despite the fact he is on a pace to score 52 goals, in contrast to the 62 and 65 he as had the last two seasons.

"It's obvious that myself, Gerard (Gallant), Jimmy Carson, we didn't get off to the start that was expected of us," said Yzerman, who believed Saturday's was his first natural hat trick. "But as long as we keep on working, things are going to come. The top players have to do their jobs, which is scoring goals. The other players are doing their jobs."

Yzerman is accustomed to the pressure of having to score. In the last two seasons, often accumulating 30 minutes or more of ice time a game, he has been the player the team has looked to for clutch goals. Saturday, he got them in a hurry.

"It's not pressure," said Yzerman, when asked if it was an unfair burden. "It's just the way it is. There are certain players who are scorers and are expected to do that.

"The goals came so early, I thought, 'Let's just keep this rolling.' But with the way things went in the second, the pace pretty much slowed down."

That was because Yzerman spent 10 minutes of the second period in the penalty box with a misconduct issued by referee Ron Hoggarth. It was the only time the Leafs actually pressed the Red Wings during the bulk of the game.

"I think it was too much Steve Yzerman in the first period," Toronto coach Tom Watt said. "The best thing that happened to us was when he got that 10-minute misconduct. That, at least, gave us some respite from them."

But in the end, the Red Wings' firepower took care of the Leafs.

Yzerman joins Chicago defenseman Chris Chelios and goalie Ed Belfour in a fight for the loose puck.

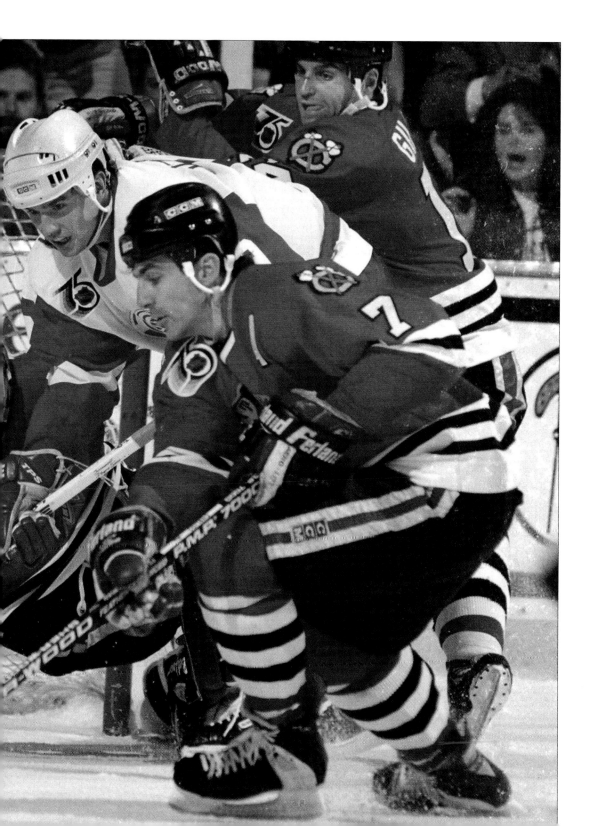

Feb. 24, 1993: Sabres 10, Wings 7

Yzerman Gets 1,000th Point

But He Can't Rescue Wings in Loss to Sabres

By Cynthia Lambert
....

The Detroit News

Buffalo, Feb. 24, 1993 — Last week when Steve Yzerman was asked how he'd feel when he registered his 1,000th career NHL point, he hesitated.

"You never know what'll happen in the game after you get the point," Yzerman said. "A lot can happen."

It proved to be a prophetic statement.

Yzerman collected his 1,000th point at 11:22 of the first period of Wednesday's game against the Sabres, when he assisted on Keith Primeau's power-play goal. But what happened after that goal was pure ugliness, as the Sabres went on to defeat the Red Wings, 10-7.

"We really played poorly," Yzerman said. "It was 10-7 but it really wasn't even close.

"It was kind of a disappointing game to get

the point in. It certainly wasn't the way I'd like to plan a milestone like this. It was somewhat anti-climatic. I mean, I'm glad I reached it, don't get me wrong. I'm glad I got it over with. But it was a difficult game to get it in. I sure didn't play terribly well and the team was about the same."

After Primeau scored the goal, Sabres goalie Grant Fuhr reached in and slid the puck out toward the blue line. Yzerman skated up to it, reached down and picked it up.

"No one else was going for it so I figured I had better," Yzerman said, smiling. "I wanted to get to it before they shot it in our net."

Primeau's goal made it a 2-1 game, with the Sabres holding the edge. Yzerman became the 37th player in NHL history to get 1,000 points.

The Sabres' tandem of Alexander Mogilny

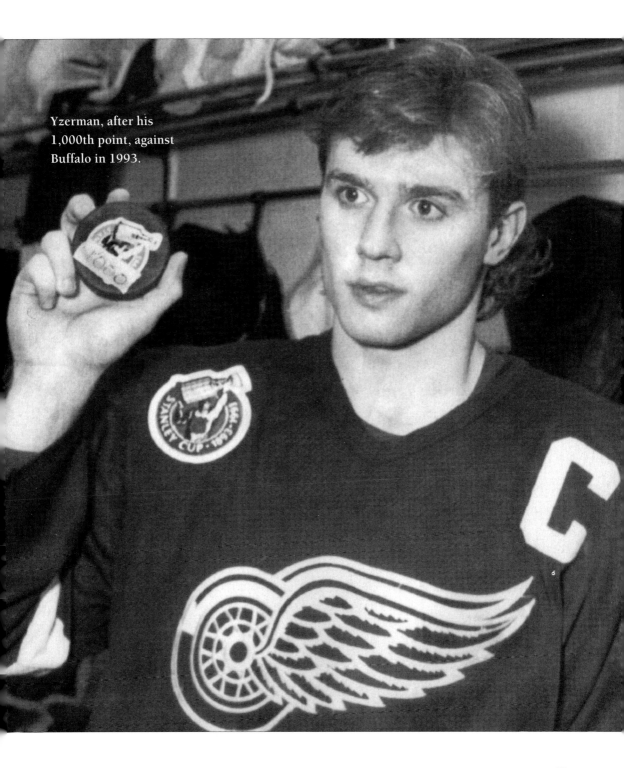

Yzerman, after his
1,000th point, against
Buffalo in 1993.

Sabres 10, Wings 7

Detroit	1	2	4	7
Buffalo	3	3	4	10

First period

1, Buffalo, Mogilny 57, 1:03. 2, Buffalo, Mogilny 58 (LaFontaine, Ramsey), 5:22. 3, Detroit, Primeau 13 (Ciccarelli, Yzerman), 11:22 (pp). 4, Buffalo, Mogilny 59 (Smehlik, LaFontaine), 17:28. Penalties—Hannan, Buf (tripping), 9:49; Primeau, Det, major (fighting), 13:54; Ray, Buf, major (fighting) 13:54; Ledyard, Buf (holding), 15:28.

Second period

5, Buffalo, Sutton 7 (May, LaFontaine). 1:06; 6, Buffalo, LaFontaine 37 (Hawerchuk) 4:44 (pp). 7, Detroit, Yzerman, 47 (Gallant, Konstantinov), 5:30. 8, Buffalo, Mogilny 60 (Hannan, Khmylev), 9:07. 9, Detroit, Ysebaert 27 (Yzerman, Sheppard), 12:54. Penalties—Chiasson, Det (tripping), 4:40; Ramsey, Buf (interference), 15:58; Howe, Det (tripping), 18:46.

Third period

10, Detroit, Drake 11 (Fedorov, Racine), 1:26. 11, Buffalo, LaFontaine 38 (Ramsey, Donnelly) 3:27. 12, Buffalo, Corkum 6 (Hannan, Ray), 4:39. 13, Detroit, Sheppard 22 (Yzerman, Howe), 5:07. 14, Detroit, Drake 12 (Fedorov), 5:50. 15, Detroit, Sheppard 23, 9:09. 16, Buffalo, Khmylev 15 (Mogilny), 10:22. 17, Buffalo, Wood 16 (Hawerchuk, Ramsey), 16:54. Penalties—none.

Shots on goal

Detroit	10	10	11	31
Buffalo	15	14	8	37

and Pat LaFontaine dominated the offense. Mogilny scored four goals and had one assist. LaFontaine had a pair of goals and three assists.

The first goal by Mogilny allowed him to break Danny Gare's record for most goals in a season by a Sabre. The old record was 56. Mogilny now has 60. Mogilny also picked up an additional $40,000. He gets $10,000 for every goal over 50 as part of his contract's bonus package.

"What can I say?" Mogilny said. "I'm the happiest man alive. I have the opportunity to play with Pat. I'm so happy."

"I asked Alex for the puck," LaFontaine said. "I told him I wanted 60. He could have the pucks after he gets his 70th and 80th goals."

The hat trick by Mogilny also tied a Sabres record for most in a season, held by Rick Martin, who had seven during the 1975-76 season.

"Pat and Mogilny played about as well as any two players I've seen," Yzerman said. "Right from the very first shift they were something else. That's the most chances I've ever seen a line have."

Yzerman also scored a goal and assisted on two other Detroit goals, giving him 1,003 total career points. Paul Ysebaert, Dallas Drake (two) and Ray Sheppard (two) scored the other Detroit goals.

Ken Sutton, Bob Corkum, Yuri Khmylev and Randy Wood scored the other goals for the Sabres.

The dreadful defensive performance by the Red Wings was something that struck a nerve in Coach Bryan Murray and a number of the players. It seems as though the team peaked during Saturday's 4-1 victory over Minnesota, and

Yzerman, the Red Wings' 3rd all-time scorer.

has been on a spiral downward ever since.

"It was an awful game," Murray said. "(The Sabres) probably could have had another four or five goals, too.

"We had been playing so much better than this. I know when you go on the road you're not going to win every night, but we can play so much better than this."

The Wings may be road weary, but they had better find a way to re-energize, considering they have another long road trip coming up after next week's two-game trip to New Jersey and Long Island.

Up In the Wings

The Red Wings' top 10 career scoring leaders:

Name	Yrs.	Pts.
Gordie Howe	25	1809
Alex Delvecchio	24	1281
Steve Yzerman	10	1003
Norm Ullman	13	758
Ted Lindsay	14	728
Reed Larson	10	570
John Ogrodnick	9	539
Nick Libett	12	467
Sid Abel	10	463
Gerard Gallant	9	456

Feb. 24, 1993

Jan. 17, 1996: Wings 3, Avalanche 2

No. 500 For The Captain

Milestone Goal Sparks Red Wings' Victory

By Cynthia Lambert

....

The Detroit News

Detroit, Jan. 17, 1996 — Steve Yzerman has been a magic man for the Red Wings since he first arrived in the summer of 1983.

And on Wednesday night, midway through his 13th season with Detroit, Yzerman created another magical moment at Joe Louis Arena when he lifted a backhand shot past Colorado goalie Patrick Roy. It was the 500th goal of his career, all scored wearing the winged wheel.

Yzerman could not stop smiling after he scored the power-play goal at 7:52 of the second to make it a 2-0 game. The Red Wings went on to win the game, 3-2.

"I wanted to score the goal in a game we won," Yzerman said. "I was so pleased that Sergei got that goal.

"Of this whole thing, the part that pleases me

most is that I've been here for the 13 years to get them. I see faces in the crowd I've recognized for 13 years, people I've met here, people who work in the building — the ones I see on the way in, and the ones I see on the way out. They've seen my whole career. They shared in this. They have the same feelings we do."

On the milestone play, Yzerman took a pass from Greg Johnson in the slot. Yzerman's initial shot was blocked by defenseman Alexei Gusarov. But the puck was bounced into the slot area, where Yzerman regrouped and lifted it over a sprawling Roy. Appropriately, the goal was No. 19 for the man who's worn No. 19 for his entire NHL career.

The fact that he got the goal against Roy made

Wings 3, Avalanche 2

Colorado	0	1	1	2
Detroit	1	1	1	3

First period

1, Detroit, Primeau 12 (Larionov), 5:19. Penalties — Rychel, Col (interference), :20; Ozolinsh, Col (cross-checking), 6:19; Ciccarelli, Det (roughing), 10:33.

Second period

2, Detroit, Yzerman 19 (Johnson, Fedorov), 7:52 (pp). 3, Colorado, Young 14, 11:17. Penalties — Klemm, Col (hooking), 6:29, Johnson, Det (hooking), 11:53, Young, Col (kneeing), 16:06.

Third period

4, Colorado, Deadmarsh 15, (Lefebvre, Sakic), 6:04. 5, Detroit, Fedorov 19 (Larionov), 11:28. Penalties — none.

Shots on goal

Colorado	6	5	8	19
Detroit	7	13	8	28

it that much more special for Yzerman.

"I hope he's happy he got it," said Roy, allowing a grin. "I'm happy for him, really. He's a good player and he's been one of the best players in the NHL for many, many years."

Yzerman said: "I don't consider it a great goal. I just threw it at the net. But I am pleased I got it against a guy like Patty. He's a Hall of Fame goalie and that makes it more special."

Immediately following the goal, the Red Wings bench emptied so players could congratulate their teammate, and goalie Chris

Yzerman salutes Red Wings fans.

Yzerman scores his 500th goal against
Colorado in 1996.

Fast Road to 500

Steve Yzerman is about to become the 22nd player in NHL history to score 500 goals. Following are the players who reached 500 goals the fastest, with number of games needed.

Player	Games
Wayne Gretzky	575
Mario Lemieux	605
Phil Esposito	803
Jari Kurri	833
Bobby Hull	861
Maurice Richard	863
Marcel Dionne	887

Dec. 21, 1995

All-time Red Wing Goal Scorers

Steve Yzerman became the second player to score 500 goals as a Red Wing when he found the net Wednesday night, Dino Ciccarelli has scored 538, but only 94 were scored with the Wings.

Player	Total
1. Gordie Howe	786
2. Steve Yzerman	500
3. Alex Delvecchio	456

Jan. 17, 1996

Fortunate 500

Listed in chronological order, the following players have scored 500 goals during their NHL careers. Included are the team with which each reached the milestone, the game in which it happened, and each player's career statistics.

Player	Team	Game No.	Total Goals	Total Games
Maurice Richard	Montreal	863	544	978
Gordie Howe	Detroit	1,045	801	1,767
Bobby Hull	Chicago	861	610	1,063
Jean Beliveau	Montreal	1,101	507	1,125
Frank Mahovlich	Montreal	1,105	533	1,181
Phil Esposito	Boston	803	717	1,282
John Bucyk	Boston	1,370	556	1,540
Stan Makita	Chicago	1,221	541	1,394
Marcel Dionne	Los Angeles	887	731	1,348
Guy Lafleur	Montreal	918	560	1,126
Mike Bossy	NY Islanders	647	573	762
Gilbert Perreault	Buffalo	1,159	512	1,191
Wayne Gretzky	Edmonton	575	823	1,206
Lanny McDonald	Calgary	1,107	500	1,111
Bryan Trottier	NY Islanders	1,104	524	1,279
Mike Gartner	NY Rangers	936	645	1,241
Michel Goulet	Chicago	951	548	1,089
Jari Kurri	Los Angeles	833	572	1,060
Dino Ciccarelli	Detroit	946	534	1,037
Mario Lemieux	Pittsburgh	605	523	626
Mark Messier	NY Rangers	1,141	514	1,163

Osgood made the long skate deep into the Colorado zone to offer his congratulations.

Meanwhile, the sellout crowd of 19,983 at Joe Louis Arena gave Yzerman a standing ovation for two minutes — a fitting soundtrack to Yzerman's celebration that continued on the bench. It was there that he received a couple of hugs from assistant coach Barry Smith, a pat on the back and handshake from Coach Scotty Bowman, and a rub on his helmet from assistant Dave Lewis.

"Leading up to the goal, I didn't know how to react to it," Yzerman said. "The players and everybody came onto the ice, we started horsing around and all that. That was the best part of the whole thing, guys rubbing their gloves in my face, me just looking at the guys' faces."

When he finally took his seat on the bench, after handing his stick over to the trainer for safe keeping, Yzerman wiped his mouth with his hand. When the hand disappeared, the smile reappeared, illustrating the impact on the usually mild-mannered Wings captain.

"All I feel is simply happiness," Yzerman said. "I used to take this game so seriously. Now I enjoy it. I'm looser."

Yzerman is the 22nd NHL player to reach 500 goals. Pittsburgh's Mario Lemieux and the New York Rangers' Mark Messier accomplished the feat earlier this season. Yzerman is the fourth Red Wing to make the 500 club. Dino Ciccarelli, who previously played for Minnesota and Washington, was the most recent, getting his on Jan. 8, 1994. Gordie Howe and Marcel Dionne are the other Red Wings to score 500. Yzerman and Howe are the only players with 500 all in a Red Wings uniform.

Yzerman Will Probably Give Away the Stick that Scored No. 500

By Cynthia Lambert

The Detroit News

It's hard to believe, but Steve Yzerman is probably going to take the stick he used to score his 500th goal and give it away. If he does, he is only following a pattern he established early on in his illustrious career.

"I'm not really sure what I'll do with it," said Yzerman, who made a point of saving the stick. "I've given most of them to friends. The one I used to get my 1,000th point, I had to give to Mrs. (Marian) Ilitch for the archives.

"I don't know. What do you do with a stick? It doesn't suit the decor of my house."

In addition to Johnson, Sergei Fedorov, playing defense, assisted on Yzerman's goal. In the final minute of the first period, Yzerman had a good shot at getting the historic goal, but was stopped by Roy. That chance, too, came on a rebound.

Detroit took a 1-0 lead earlier in the first when Keith Primeau scored his 12th of the season, at 5:19.

The goal was Primeau's second in three games, and in the last game he left early with a bruised left kneecap.

Yzerman's goal gave the Wings some padding when, at 11:17 of the second period Scott Young beat Osgood low to make the score 2-1 entering the third period.

That cushion disappeared at 6:04 of the third, when Adam Deadmarsh deflected a Sylvain Lefebvre shot from the right point to make it 2-2.

Until the third period, the Wings had been relatively successful in containing the slick-skating Avalanche. Through two periods, Colorado had 11 shots on net, two less than the Red Wings took in the second period alone.

But from the start of the third, the Avalanche pressed for shots and took some dandies at Osgood.

Once again, because Slava Fetisov was in Moscow attending to personal matters, and Mike Ramsey was injured, Fedorov played defense, which has become his new position. But that isn't where he was playing when he scored the goal to make it 3-2. In a great individual effort to draw Roy out of position, Fedorov, playing right wing, took a pass from linemate Igor Larionov, then faked a shot before moving to the left and shooting into the net. The goal was Fedorov's 19th of the season.

Yzerman, is congratulated by his teammates after his 500th goal.

Electrifying Score Thrusts Second-Chance Captain Back Into the Limelight

By Bob Wojnowski

....

The Detroit News

He shot the puck and then didn't quit. He dug and poked at the rebound, scooped it up, went to the backhand and lifted the puck that lifted the weight, and lifted the crowd.

The puck found the net, and Steve Yzerman found his moment, fittingly and finally. The captain who reinvented his style to help his team, scored on a rebound 7:52 into the second period Wednesday night in the Wings' 3-2 victory against Colorado, joining 21 other NHL luminaries with 500 goals. The second-chance guy scored another second-chance goal, a product of grit and hustle, a testament to perseverance.

These are the moments that make sports special. Joe Louis Arena shook as it seldom has. The two-minute standing ovation should be framed, the thunderous noise shook the ice as teammates swarmed Yzerman. He emerged from the mob wearing a smile we've rarely seen. He raised a fist, skated to the bench and then tried, in vain, to wipe the elation from his face.

"I wouldn't say it was relief, because I've enjoyed the tension," Yzerman said 30 minutes later, the smile still affixed. "It was simply happiness."

Few athletes in this town have seen more and done more and been rewarded less than Yzerman. He was the franchise's only jewel during the darkest years, then seemingly a spare part during the recent bright years. He has endured injury and indignation, the subject of ridiculous trade rumors, pushed from position to position by the newest hotshots.

Yzerman had tried mightily to downplay the significance of the milestone, but as the tally mounted, so did the excitement. And when the goal came and you saw the smile and heard the "Stevie! Stevie!" chant, you knew what it meant. He became only the seventh player to score 500 goals with the same team.

"The first 499 goals were to help the team win," center Keith Primeau said. "No. 500 was for him."

It was a moment more emotional even than opening night, when the crowd saluted its captain. It was a moment that rivaled the one last spring, when Yzerman skated with the conference cup after the Red Wings beat Chicago.

The smile wouldn't end and neither would the applause. This is a guy utterly unaffected by almost everything. On this night, the veneer melted.

"I've never seen that smile before," said Dino Ciccarelli, who joined the 500 club two years ago.

"He's such a serious guy, such a hard worker. He'll blow it off like it was no big deal, but that smile was different."

Today, we see a different player, a man tested by adversity, driven to win. How many stars would completely alter their games in their 12th or 13th seasons? Yzer-man, once one of the league's premier scorers, now is one of its top two-way players, executing the Red Wings' defensive system with passion and precision.

He is more feisty, more willing to deliver a hit, or a punch.

He leads this team by following orders, by making second-chance plays after a career as a first-chance guy.

Against Colorado, Yzerman got into skirmishes again, went low to block a shot, sacrificed his body. This is why the Red Wings are so good, because none of their players are too good. Sergei Fedorov, a former MVP center, played on defense much of the game to compensate for injuries and absences.

When it was over, after all the attention and most of the interview, Yzerman stood in front of his locker to greet a visitor.

"I was glad to see history," said Colts quarterback Jim Harbaugh, a second-chance guy who knows all about rebounds. Harbaugh shook hands with Yzerman, who just kept smiling, a look that said more than we'll ever know.

Yzerman duels with Colorado's Claude Lemieux.

Yzerman chases after St. Louis' Adam Creighton.

May 5, 1996: Wings 8, Blues 3

Yzerman Ties Record

He Gets Five Points to Match Ullman's Playoff Feat

By Cynthia Lambert

The Detroit News

Detroit, May 5, 1996 — Scoring three goals against the Red Wings in a playoff game generally would produce results. That is, unless you're the St. Louis Blues and your goaltender gives up five goals in the first period.

The ugly result was an 8-3 Red Wings victory over the Blues on Sunday afternoon for a two-games-to-none lead in the best-of-seven series. Games 3 and 4 will be Wednesday and Friday at the Kiel Center.

"He was awful," Blues coach Mike Keenan

Wings 8, Blues 3

St. Louis	1	1	1	3
Detroit	5	0	3	8

First period

1, Detroit, Yzerman 3 (Errey), 3:40. 2, Detroit, Konstantinov 2 (Larionov, Fedorov), 4:45. 3, Detroit, Lidstrom 1 (Yzerman) 7:02. 4, Detroit, McCarty 2 (Yzerman), 11:41. 5, St. Louis, Corson 7 (Gretzky, Pronger), 13:27 (pp). 6, Detroit, Lapointe 1 (draper), 15:40. Penalties — Pronger, StL (slashing), 1:34; Ciccarelli, Det (interference), 8:46; Fetisov, Det (holding stick), 13:25; Leach, StL (interference), 18:31, Konstantinov, Det (interference), 19:57.

Second period

7, St. Louis, Zezel 3 (Anderson, Courtnall), 2:48. Penalties — Anderson, StL (tripping), 3:27; Creighton, StL, (interference), 7:25; Pronger, StL (roughing), 9:04; MacTavish, StL (roughing), 12:45; Coffey, Det (roughing), 12:45; Draper, Det (interference), 18:42; Konstantinov, Det (roughing), 19:19.

Third period

8, Detroit, Lidstrom 2 (Coffey, Yzerman), 6:19 (pp). 9, St. Louis, Creighton, 1 (Kravchuk), 8:03. 10, Detroit, Yzerman 4 (Errey, Fetisov), 17:56 (pp). 11, Detroit, Bergevin 1 (Taylor), 19:35 (pp). Penalties — Courtnall, StL (high-sticking), 1:36; Baron, StL (high-sticking), 4:44; Lapointe, Det (tripping), 9:42. Leach, StL (roughing), 12:56; MacInnis, StL, (interference), 14:16; Corson, StL (slashing), 15:22; Baron, StL (high-sticking), 17:13; Twist, StL (roughing), 17:56; Corson, double-minor (roughing), 17:56; McCarty, Det (roughing) 17;56; Konstantinov, Det (roughing), 17:56; Casey, StL, served by Pronger (interference), 18:52.

Shots on goal

St. Louis	6	8	7	21
Detroit	11	7	13	31

said of goaltender Jon Casey.

The most repulsive part of the game for the Blues was the first 11:41, when Casey gave up four goals on nine shots. The Wings weren't lobbing beach balls at Casey, but a couple of the goals could have been prevented with a bit of defense and a better reaction from Casey.

"I think we caught them a bit flat-footed," Bob Errey said. "We rolled out lines pretty quick early on. It must have been like getting hit with five punches in a row. It's hard to recuperate."

Steve Yzerman, Vladimir Konstantinov, Nick Lidstrom and Darren McCarty scored by 11:41 of the first. After that, Casey was replaced by play-

Yzerman listens to advice from his coach, Scotty Bowman.

off rookie Bruce Racine — for 33 seconds. While on the bench, Casey tried to compose himself.

It didn't work.

The Blues' Shayne Corson (power play) and the Red Wings' Martin Lapointe also scored in the first, and the Red Wings led, 5-1, entering the second period. Peter Zezel's goal in the second made it 5-2 entering the third. Lidstrom and the Blues' Adam Creighton traded goals to make it 6-3. Yzerman and Marc Bergevin scored on the power play for the final margin.

Yzerman assisted on two goals, giving him

five points and tying Norm Ullman's team record for most points in a playoff game.

"I don't get too excited by one game," Yzerman said.

The rest of the Red Wings apparently are following their captain's lead. Winning by five goals in one game doesn't necessarily mean the rest of the series will be a breeze. But since Casey is the Blues' only option in goal, that may be just what it means.

"They're not desperate right now," said Kris Draper, giving the Blues the benefit of the doubt. "But I guess you could say their backs are against the wall."

Steve Yzerman

Yzerman addresses
reporters before
the 1996 playoffs.

Yzerman Concerned About Present, Not Red Wings' Past Playoff Failures

By Jerry Green

The Detroit News

For 13 seasons in Detroit, the rap has been on Steve Yzerman.

The crowds love him, cheer him boisterously, but when the playoffs begin, the sour-grape artists emerge, wailing:

"Stevie doesn't do it in the playoffs."

During some springtimes, he has been seriously injured. A year ago, he played despite a bum knee. In the spring of 1988, he missed 13 games because of a torn knee ligament and returned for the Edmonton Oilers series. Rather than applaud him for his courage, hockey fans condemned him because the Red Wings lost.

Even this year, a caller using the captivating medium of sports-talk radio trashed Yzerman on WDFN: "He's having another lousy playoffs."

Yzerman used his own forum — TV networks in two nations — to respond to critics Sunday. Hockey fans in the United States and Canada watched Yzerman get two goals and three assists in the Red Wings' rout of the St. Louis Blues.

Whatever the demons, he proved again that he could lead and play winning playoff hockey.

"I'm not so much concerned with proving anything," Yzerman said in characteristic understatement.

"I don't concern myself with (fans' griping). I've learned to deal with that, accept that. I go out, do my best and believe that at some time things will work out."

Yzerman has been the captain with the C on his jersey for 10 years. In those seasons, he watched team captains such as Wayne Gretzky and Mario Lemieux circle hockey rinks in other towns with the Stanley Cup raised to a multitude of cheers. They are athletes of his ilk, and Yzerman has spoken at times about how he listened in his car radio to the Stanley Cup presentation and dreamed.

"I hope to get that opportunity now," he said. "We'll keep working at it."

Yzerman's five points put him in the team record book. He tied Normie Ullman for the most points in a playoff game by a Red Wing. Ullman twice had five points against the Chicago Blackhawks in the 1960s.

Keenan's Message Loses Something in the Translation; His Team Looks Feeble

By Bob Wojnowski
....

The Detroit News

Speaking of dives ...were those the St. Louis Bluehairs stumbling around Joe Louis Arena Sunday?

Speaking of disgraces ... was that Mike Keenan getting out-dimwitted?

Speaking of flops ... was that Blues goalie Jon Casey battling the puck like a drunk trying to stomp a roach?

Speaking of bad acting ... was that Wayne Gretzky impersonating an aging superstar?

That's about it on the questions. If Keenan wishes to start any more controversies, rile any more Red Wings, he's nuttier than we thought. The challenge now for the Red Wings — ahead, 2-0, in the series after their 8-3 pummeling of St. Louis — is to stay interested long enough to win two more games.

Keenan, mental munchkin, chose the wrong time to pick a fight. These Red Wings simply don't get distracted, not by a tough opener, not by tough goalies, not by Keenan's suggestion that Sergei Fedorov is "a disgrace to the NHL."

"We didn't pay any attention to it whatsoever,"

said Steve Yzerman, who tied a team playoff record with five points. "We didn't play particularly well the other night, and we wanted to be sharper. That's it. The other stuff is irrelevant. We play the team, not the coach."

It's irrelevant because the Wings rendered it so. But Keenan's diatribe underscored the Blues' frustration after they played so well in the opener and the Red Wings played so poorly, yet won.

Fifteen minutes into Game 2, the Red Wings had fired 11 shots, scored five goals and delivered a pointed response to lame questions. Besides blistering Fedorov for allegedly faking injuries, Keenan spouted tired cliches about the differences between Russian players and North American players, an ugly bias that really needs to die.

Honestly, few of the Red Wings cared what Keenan said. They just went out and attacked poor Casey. Yzerman stuffed an early goal, setting the tone, unlocking the barrage. Casey at the bat? Nah. Casey on the mat. Keenan pulled him briefly, then sent him back out. Afterward,

Wayne Gretzky (front) checks the time remaining in the game.

he called Casey "awful," probably because "disgrace" had been used.

This series essentially ended when St. Louis goalie Grant Fuhr suffered a knee injury in the previous round. The Blues can't skate with the Red Wings, can't bang the Red Wings. If the Red Wings were sluggish in the opener, Keenan made sure everyone was awake for Game 2. Well, everyone but the Blues' ailing stars, Gretzky and Brett Hull.

I'm not saying Gretzky has been conspicuously absent. I'm just saying it's easier to find Fox's glowing puck than it is to find the Grey One, still without a goal in these playoffs. The snapshot of Gretzky's frustration came in the third period, at the end of a Blues two-man advantage. Alone in front of the net, Gretzky feebly slid the puck into Chris Osgood's pads, then skated away slowly, head down.

From there, the Red Wings got bored, and the Blues got stupid. Disgrace? How about the third-period fiasco, when St. Louis committed 11 penalties, including a mugging of Bob Errey by Casey himself, who finally found something he could keep out of the net.

"We just shrug it off," Red Wings forward Tim Taylor said. "Their actions reflected their coach. How bad is that? That's just Mike Keenan hockey."

Hmm. Maybe it was another of those famous messages Keenan likes to send.

"We don't send messages that way," Dino Ciccarelli said. "We do it on the scoreboard."

The scoreboard told the story, explicitly and predictably. You try to distract these Wings, you're wasting your time. Keenan and the Blues are learning the hard way.

After his 5-point performance,
Yzerman greets the Red
Wings fans.

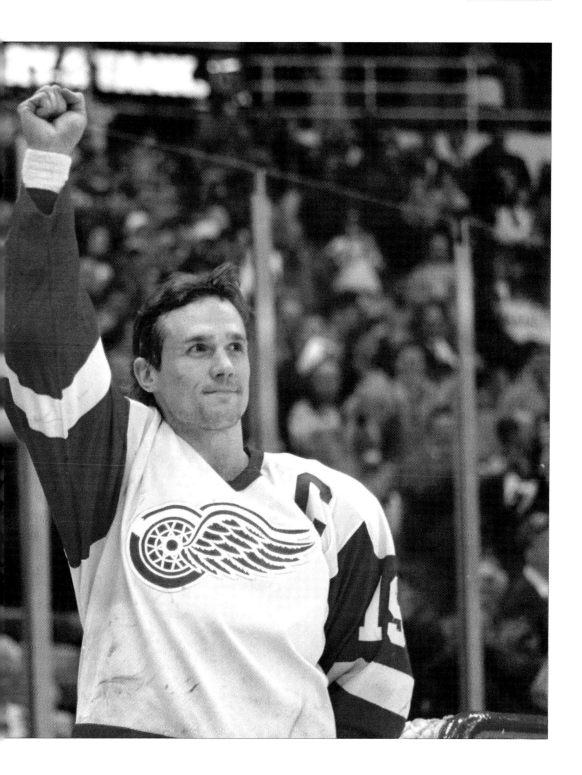

Yzerman celebrates with his teammates after defeating St. Louis in the 1996 playoffs.

May 16, 1996: Wings 1, Blues 0

Yzerman to the Rescue

Goal in Second Overtime Beats the Blues

By Cynthia Lambert

The Detroit News

Detroit, May 16, 1996 — The irony was inescapable.

"He kept saying he didn't care who scored and he's the one who did," said Red Wings coach Scotty Bowman of Steve Yzerman's goal 1:15 into the second overtime Thursday night.

The goal gave the Red Wings a 1-0 victory over the St. Louis Blues in Game 7 of the Western Conference semifinals.

It was the Red Wings' first victory in a Game 7 in three recent tries. They lost in 1994 to San Jose and in 1993 to Toronto. Granted, it took double-overtime, but the Wings will take it.

The goal, scored on Yzerman's eighth shot of the night, not only gave the Red Wings the victory, but enabled them to advance to the Western Conference finals against the Colorado

Avalanche. The series begins at 3 p.m. Sunday at Joe Louis Arena.

"Yeah, that's the most exciting goal I've scored," said Yzerman, the Red Wings' top playoff scorer with eight goals and 17 points.

The shutout was goaltender Chris Osgood's second of the playoffs.

"It feels good, that's all," Osgood said. "I think a win like this shows that this team has grown. There was no negative thinking going on."

Vladimir Konstantinov sent Yzerman in when he made a long pass to the Detroit captain through the neutral zone.

Wayne Gretzky nearly intercepted the pass, but once the puck got to Yzerman, he was off and skating. When he passed the blue line on the right side, he let loose a shot that beat goalie

Jon Casey high.

"I didn't have great speed, but I had some," Yzerman said. "I felt I could get it away. I wasn't thinking score, I was thinking of getting it by the defensemen."

"I know the play was to get it in deep, but I did have some speed and I wanted to get a shot away."

And away it went. The scene was a flash compared to the prime scoring chances the Red Wings had during the game.

One of their best opportunities came just 14 seconds into the second overtime when Yzerman skated behind the net and shuffled the puck to Sergei Fedorov in the slot. But Casey made the save.

The Wings outshot the Blues, 40-29.

Wings 1, Blues 0

St. Louis	0	0	0	0	0	0
Detroit	0	0	0	0	1	1

First period

None. Penalties — MacInnis, StL (tripping), 7:47; Kravchuk, StL, (interference), 11:04; Draper, Det (holding), 13:56; Leach, StL, (boarding), 17:51.

Second period

None. Penalty — Ramsey, Det (interference) 5:28.

Third period

None. Penalties — none.

Overtime

None. Penalties — none.

Second overtime

1, Detroit, Yzerman 8 (Konstantinov), 1:15. Penalties — none.

Shots

St. Louis	4	11	6	8	0	29
Detroit	14	6	12	6	2	40

Yzerman's double overtime goal ensured the Red Wings' playoff victory over the Blues.

Osgood's Outstanding Performance Sets Up Yzerman for Game-Winner

By Terry Foster

....

The Detroit News

Left wing Shayne Corson had Red Wings goalie Chris Osgood right where he wanted him.

Corson tamed a rowdy puck after stripping defenseman Vladimir Konstantinov and skated in alone on Osgood with 6:57 left in the first overtime of Thursday's Game 7 epic between the Wings and the Blues.

Corson fired a wicked slap shot, but Osgood threw his body in front of the puck as if it were a live grenade and slapped it out of harm's way with his trusty stick.

Osgood was dead — left hanging by his defense. Plain and simple. No doubt about it.

"To tell you the truth, I don't remember that play," Osgood said. "It was such a long game."

Steve Yzerman became the hero of this 81-minute, 15-second double-overtime 1-0 Red Wings victory. But Yzerman would have never gotten the chance if not for Osgood.

He worked a miracle on the Corson shot, just as he did in the first period when he reached back to stop a missile off the stick of Brian Noonan.

"I didn't remember that one either," Osgood said.

So that's what happens when you hit a zone. The entire game becomes a blur, a flash of whizzing pucks and arms and legs and sticks.

You don't remember. And no one else forgets.

This was a classic at the Joe Louis Arena, one we will store in our memory banks for years to come. It erases that horrible memory of Osgood attempting to clear the puck in Game 7 of the San Jose series in 1994. Osgood grew into a man that night. The hockey world saw his maturity on Thursday.

And how about a kind word for his counterpart, Jon Casey, who pitched a perfect game until Yzerman's shot skimmed over his right shoulder and into the net. Every shot and every deflection meant life and death for Casey and Osgood.

The little men of this series played bigger than anyone. It was only appropriate that after 80 minutes and 67 shots of this Game 7 drama, the score remained 0-0.

Isn't it funny. Before the season began, both men were slated for backup roles.

Red Wings coach Scotty Bowman appeared to be more comfortable with Mike Vernon until

Whew! Yzerman 1, Blues 0

They tried and tried and tried.

Finally, Red Wings captain Steve Yzerman took charge like he has so many times this season and put the puck in the net at 1:15 of the second overtime.

"It was a tremendous thrill," Yzerman said. "It's what all players dream about."

The Red Wings' 1-0 victory left Detroit fans filled with joy in Joe Louis Arena on Thursday night.

"I Want Stanley" is still the song to sing in Motown.

Goalie Chris Osgood kept the Wings in the game time after time as both teams played hard up and down the ice. "It was one of the most exciting things I've been a part of," Osgood said.

Detroit won the best-of-seven series, 4-3, after falling behind, 3-2.

Maybe peeking at the Blues' scouting report helped.

Now the Red Wings take on the Colorado Avalanche at 3 p.m. Sunday in Joe Louis Arena.

The Red Wings haven't won the Stanley Cup since 1955. That 41-year drought is the longest in the NHL. But the gritty comeback from a 3-2 deficit in this series had Coach Scotty Bowman thinking this might by the year.

All they need to do now is win eight more.

Osgood outplayed him.

Osgood stopped everything that came his way. Osgood?

How about Os-gr-r-r-e-e-a-a-t-t!

"It felt good out there," Osgood said. "I felt like I was in a groove. I saw the puck well. I said 'Let's get one. We are going to win. Enough is enough.'"

The Red Wings' defense was just as sharp. Sure, there were a couple of lapses, but when games last this long, someone is bound to fall asleep at the switch.

Actually, the Red Wings' bench made the defensive play of the game during the first overtime after Nicklas Lidstrom broke his stick on a slapshot from the point.

The Blues were headed for a certain three-on-one break. As Lidstrom skated by the Red Wings' bench, someone alertly handed him a stick and Lidstrom used that piece of lumber to break up the play.

There was tension from the opening faceoff, which of course, is no fun for fretting Red Wings fans. You may have felt it, but Osgood felt none of the tension in the air.

"It's fun. I love it," he said. "I'm sure a lot of the guys in here loved it. We were not nervous. Everybody has been through it."

For the last line of defense, it became a game of who would blink first. That is what we waited nearly four hours to see.

Time seemed to stand still as the Wizard of Oz turned in a performance we won't soon forget.

"It was one of the most exciting things I've been a part of," Osgood said.

We feel the same way.

Red Wings Had Luck on Their Side

By Cynthia Lambert
....

The Detroit News

Red Wings assistant coach Barry Smith said he never wavered.

"Actually, I felt really good today going into this game," Smith said after the Red Wings' 1-0 double-overtime victory over the Blues.

Smith's comments were echoed by many Detroit players. But when the whole thing boils down to a Game 7 with a heavily-favored team going against an underdog featuring some of the best players in NHL history, anything can happen.

But "anything" didn't happen. The better team won in a fashion so dramatic it left some of its players breathless.

"I'm so tired," defenseman Paul Coffey said. "A bounce going the other way and we could have been sitting here talking about how tough a loss it was.

"It's so strange. Just less than two weeks ago we were up 2-0 in the series. Then earlier this week, the whole city wants to kill you. That's playoffs. This series ranks right up there with the Chicago series last year. It proves if we play our best hockey we can do it."

The Red Wings were a deflection or a freak bounce away from elimination. And they know it.

"It's a real tough day tomorrow if you lose," Coach Scotty Bowman said. "It's the end of the world. It's not, but it feels like it."

To a man, the responses from Red Wings players were not so much of relief, but of closure.

"We were prepared for anything," Steve Yzerman said. "We were determined to win. We responded in a tough situation, and it gives us more confidence now. Ideally, you don't want to get into those situations, but eventually we expected a situation like this. We knew it."

But there is no right way to prepare for double-overtime in Game 7. There is no way to lay out a blueprint for victory in situations so tenuous.

"We always heard the first and second series were the toughest," Dino Ciccarelli said. "We believe it. But we maintained our focus. I think some people expected a little easier ride for us, but we didn't."

The Red Wings are maturing these days. As the playoff beards grow, so does the team's experience. This latest victory serves two purposes. First, it gives them confidence. Second, it shows them exactly what they need to avoid when they play Colorado.

Yzerman, savoring a special victory, talks to the media about his winning shot.

When the Wings Needed a Savior, the Captain Came Through

By Bob Wojnowski

The Detroit News

All night long, they searched for a hero. Who would end the unbelievable tension? In sudden death, who would provide sudden life?

The Red Wings got the answer they craved, when they had to have it, from Steve Yzerman, Captain with a Cause. The man had led them this far. In the wee hours of Thursday night, he took them a little farther.

Yzerman's goal, on a wicked slap shot 1:15 into the second overtime, gave the Wings a 1-0 victory over St. Louis, capping a night of remarkable drama. Has there been a more pressurized hockey game in this town in, oh, 41 years? Has there ever been a more fitting finish?

All series, Yzerman was the man who dragged this team along for the fight. As his shot whistled past goalie Jon Casey, sending the Joe Louis Arena crowd into frenzied celebration, Yzerman leaped as if dancing on air. The weight was lifted, the pressure relieved, at least for now.

Yzerman celebrates Darren McCarty's goal in Game 4.

"Everyone dreams of shots like that," he said, his hair matted with sweat. "I was stunned it went in. But you know, we never really thought we'd lose. We talked about believing in our team. If anything, our will has gotten stronger, our confidence has grown."

This is the only way to win championships. You must be tested, you must pass the test. The Red Wings were tested and taxed beyond reason, and now who knows how far they can go?

They have their most important star, Yzerman, playing the hockey of his life. He scored six goals against a gritty St. Louis team that played suffocating, frustrating defense. The Red Wings also have a goalie, Chris Osgood, playing splendidly.

One and Only

Charting the Red Wings' 1-0 overtime games in the Stanley Cup playoffs:

Date	Winning team	Losing team	Goal scorer	Time of goal
April 10, 1934	Chicago	Detroit	Mush March	10:05, 2nd OT
March 24, 1936	Detroit	Montreal	Mud Bruneteau	16:30, 6th OT
March 26, 1939	Detroit	Montreal	Marty Barry	7;47, 1st OT
April 21, 1945	Detroit	Toronto	Ed Bruneteau	14:16, 1st OT
April 9, 1950	Detroit	Toronto	Leo Reise	8:39, 1st OT
March 29, 1951	Montreal	Detroit	Maurice Richard	2:20, 3rd OT
April 28, 1992	Detroit	Minnesota	Sergei Fedorov	16:13, 1st OT
May 16, 1996	Detroit	St. Louis	Steve Yzerman	1:15, 2nd OT

If Yzerman was the ultimate hero, Osgood was the constant hero, matching Casey, save for save, as the teams skated through the thick fog of pressure, missing opportunity after opportunity.

It's the time of year when stars step up, when leaders lead. Osgood is stepping up. Yzerman is leading. After Red Wings lost Game 5, Yzerman stood up and said they would win the next one, then gave the effort that made it possible, He deflected criticism from the team's struggling scorers. He took it all on — the physical play, the questions — without wincing or mincing words.

"He's brought his determination and leadership to another level," Dino Ciccarelli said. "It's really rubbing off on the other guys. You couldn't write a better script."

As the Wings advance and the bandwagon — tires repaired, engine tuned, seats added — rolls to the Western Conference finals against Colorado, we must acknowledge the men under the most pressure. Yzerman and Scotty Bowman took charge when they had to, before the Wings slipped into bad habits.

Both stared down the tension and delivered, and there is no doubt the Red Wings will be better and tougher for surviving.

"You have to have adversity," Bowman said. "I'm a big believer that you have to be serious, but that you have to keep your team loose."

That was Bowman's message all week, and Yzerman hammered it. The team somehow stayed relaxed, and passed the test that previous Red Wings teams have failed. The seventh-game losses in 1993 and 1994 are bad memories, not omens, because the Red Wings never abandoned their defensive system, because they learned from their mistakes, because their leader didn't let them panic.

"We proved to ourselves how to handle tough situations," Yzerman said. "We knew we were too good a team to be in this situation. Instead of being tentative, we responded to the challenge."

The captain responded, first and last, launching the shot that sent the Red Wings spiraling onward, maybe upward.

Steve Yzerman Career Highlights

- Second on team all-time list in goals
- Third in scoring
- Third in assists
- 1,000th point with assist Feb. 24, 1993
- 1,100th point with goal March 4, 1994
- Led team in points eight times
- Led team in goals six times
- Led team in assists eight times

- Scored 50 or more goals five times
- Topped 100-point mark six times (one of 13 in NHL history to do it six times in a row)
- Scored 60 goals twice
- Reached 50-goal mark in fewer games (55 in 1988-89) than any other Red Wing
- Had 18 regular-season hat tricks (recent Feb. 14, 1993, at Chicago)

A Yzerman fan celebrates the Red Wings' record-setting 61st win in May 1996.

- Had three "natural" hat tricks (recent Nov. 17, 1990, at Toronto)
- 138 career power play goals
- Club record 43 shorthand goals
- 1988-89 Lester B. Pearson Award as top performer (third in Hart Trophy that year)
- Set club records in goals, assists, and points in 1988-89 (third in NHL in each)
- In 1989-90, was second in NHL in goals, third in points
- In 1992-93, was fourth in league scoring, shared lead in short handed goals (7)

- Set club record 28-game scoring streak (29-36—65), Nov. 1—Jan. 4, 1988-89
- Two six-pointers (2-4 March 15, 1989, at Edmonton; 2-4 Feb. 16, 1990, vs. Philadelphia)
- Club record nine-game goal streak (12 total Nov. 18-Dec. 5, 1988, 14 Jan. 29-Feb. 12, 1992)
- Three for five on penalty shots
- Youngest captain (21) in team history in 1986-87
- 1983-84 Calder Trophy runnerup
- Named top rookie by the Sporting News
- 1984 Canada Cup
- 1985, '89, '90 World Champions

About the Authors

John U. Bacon, 32, was born and raised in Ann Arbor, where he attended Huron High School and the University of Michigan. He taught high school history, coached hockey and free-lanced for *The Ann Arbor Observer, Motor Trend, Bride's* and other magazines before accepting his current position at *The Detroit News.* He recently co-authored the book, *A Legacy of Champions.*

Joe Falls, 68, became a columnist for *The Detroit News* in 1978 after more than two decades of writing sports in Detroit. His career, which began with The Associated Press in New York City, spans five decades. He was born and raised in New York and also worked for the AP in Detroit, *The Detroit Times* and *The Detroit Free Press.* Falls has written six books, including *Daly Life: Memoirs of a World-Champion Coach,* about Detroit Pistons coach Chuck Daly. His other books dealt with former Michigan football coach Bo Schembechler, the Boston Marathon and the Detroit Tigers. He recently co-authored the book, *A Legacy of Champions,* a biography on University of Michigan football coaches Fielding Yost, Fritz Crisler and Bo Schembechler.

Terry Foster, 37, is a columnist for *The Detroit News.* Before his promotion in 1993, Foster covered the University of Michigan football beat and the NBA Detroit Pistons for *The News.* Foster is a native Detroiter — he's a graduate of Detroit Cass Tech High School — who has experienced both the good and bad times that is the fabric of this city's professional sports history. His ties to the community give him a different perspective than other writers who were not raised in Detroit. Foster, a graduate of Central Michigan University, has also written for *The Grand Rapids (Mich.) Press* and *The Detroit Free Press.*

Vartan Kupelian, 47, a veteran of 29 years of sportswriting, has reported on each of Detroit's professional teams since joining *The Detroit News* staff in 1971. He has also covered the championship game in each professional sport, including the World Series, Super Bowl, NBA Finals and Stanley Cup Finals. Kupelian, a graduate of Wayne State University in Detroit, has attended the last five Olympics — in Seoul, South Korea; Albertville, France; Barcelona, Spain; Lillehammer, Norway; and Atlanta. Kupelian currently covers golf for *The News.*

Cynthia Lambert, 34, has covered the Detroit Red Wings for *The Detroit News* since 1987, longer than any sportswriter currently on the hockey beat in Detroit. Her connections throughout the National Hockey League has helped her break several stories for *The News* over the years, giving *The Detroit News* the inside track in professional hockey coverage. Lambert is a 1986 graduate of Wayne State University.

Photo Credits

Allsport Photography USA: *20*

Tom Pidgeon: *front cover*

The Detroit News: *front cover, back cover, i, iv-v, 8-9, 12-13, 16, 17, 19, 23, 24-25, 26, 27, 28, 29, 30-31, 34, 35, 36, 38, 39, 41, 43, 44-45, 51, 52-53, 55, 56-57, 58-59, 61, 62-63, 65, 66-67, 69, 70, 72, 74-75, 76-77, 79, 80, 83, 85, 86-87, 89, 91, 93, 94-95, 96-both, 98-99, 101, 102-103, 104-105, 106, 109, 110-111, 112, 114-115, 119, 120, 122-123, 128*

Anita Pefley: *iii, 47, 48*

Wide World Photo: *15, 32*

About the Editor

Francis J. Fitzgerald, 38, is a noted sports researcher and editor. He has recently edited the book and video box set, Hail to the Victors: Greatest Moments in Michigan Football History (1995), and the books, The Nebraska Football Legacy (1995), That Championship Season: The 1995 Northwestern Wildcats' Road to the Rose Bowl; Greatest Moments in Penn State Football History (1996) and Greatest Moments in Steelers History (1996).